Mastering Psychology:

Discover the Science behind Motivation, Productivity and Success

(Overcome Procrastination and Laziness)

Table of Contents

Introduction   **15**

Chapter 1 – Understanding Motivation and Productivity   **18**

A Basic Concept 19

An Impact on the Entire Individual 19

What Does It Mean to Be Productive? 20

A Consistent Process 20

A Necessity for Health 21

An Indirect Point 22

Goal-Oriented 22

Different from Other Concepts 23

The Overall Goal of Motivation 26

Chapter 2 – Why Is Motivation so Important?   **28**

Managing Resources Well 28

Added Productivity 29

Establish Strong Relationships 30

A Sense of Stability 30

A Need to Attain Goals 31

A Sense of Esteem 32

Chapter 3 – A Basic Cycle 33

Four Vital Steps...33

Chapter 4 – The Three Key Parts of Motivation 37

Activation 38

Intensity..39

Persistence 39

Chapter 5 – Managing Both Desires 41

Fundamental Desires...41

Ego-Based Desires 42

Chapter 6 – Maslow's Theory of Needs and Wants 44

Physiological..45

Safety..47

Love 49

Esteem...51

Self-Actualization...52

Does This Have to Work in Order? 53

How Businesses Can Use the Pyramid 54

The Value of Meta motivation 55

Chapter 7 – The Jonah Complex (A Fear of Success) 58

Background...59

Common Signs 59

General Fears 63

How to Get Beyond the Jonah Complex 64

How Long Does It Take? 70

Chapter 8 – The ERG Theory   71

The Three Parts 72

What Makes the ERG Theory Different? 73

How This Can Be Used In the Workplace 76

How Can the Three Sections Link To Each Other? 77

Chapter 9 – Theories X and Y   79

The Basics 79

Theory X 80

Theory Y 82

Chapter 10 – The Two-Factor Theory   85

Motivators 85

Hygiene Factors 86

How Can Motivational Factors Be Increased? 88

Should Not Be Treated As a Universal Theory 89

Other Limits 90

Chapter 11 – The 16 Basic Desires   91

The Desires 92

The Reiss Profile 98

Chapter 12 – Resistance   101

A General Review of Resistance 101

Three Vital Aspects of Resistance..................................... 102

Overcoming Resistance 106

Chapter 13 – Understanding Willpower and the Link to Motivation   108

Producing a Healthy Routine.. 109

Review What's Important At the Start.................................. 110

Get Rid of Unnecessary Stuff... 110

Chapter 14 – Cognitive Motivation   112

Understanding Cognitive Psychology................................... 112

General Concepts 112

Chapter 15 – Intrinsic Motivation   115

All About Happiness 115

Creativity Is Vital.. 116

Overjustification 117

Signs a Person Is Intrinsically Motivated 117

How to Cater to Intrinsically Motivated People 119

Chapter 16 – Extrinsic Motivation 121

Rewards.. 122

Signs That Someone Is Extrinsically Motivated................................. 123

Can Extrinsic Motivation Fail?... 124

Best When a Person Shows Struggles To Do Something 125

How Long Should a Person Be Extrinsically Motivated?...................... 125

Chapter 17 – Arousal Theory 127

The Value of Dopamine.. 127

Every Person Has a Different Arousal Level 128

Can Arousal Impact Performance? (The Yerkes-Dodson Law)........... 130

Chapter 18 – The Incentive Theory 135

How This Works 135

Making Things Pleasant.. 137

Common Types of Rewards... 138

Getting Away from Negative Events 139

Can Rewards Help People Stop Behaving In a Certain Way?.............. 140

Everything Has to Be Obtainable 141

Negative Incentives.. 142

Chapter 19 – Expectancy Theory 144

Four Key Factors.. 144

Valence 145

Expectancy.. 147

Instrumentality 149

What Is the Final Motivational Force? 150

Chapter 20 – Equity Theory   152

How This Works.. 152

Moderating Variables.. 154

Chapter 21 – Goal-Setting Theory   156

What Makes the Theory Special?... 156

Important Points to Note 157

Chapter 22 – Developmental Perspectives on Motivation   159

Nature vs. Nurture... 160

The Development of the Senses... 162

The Development of the Brain 163

The Development of Neurotransmitters and Hormones 164

Chapter 23 – Piaget's Values for Cognitive Development   166

Four Key Stages 166

The Development of Ethics 168

Chapter 24 – Self-Determination Theory   171

The Three Basic Needs 171

How This Links to Intrinsic and Extrinsic Motivation 173

Chapter 25 – The Concept of Positive Psychology on Motivation 176

Concentration on the Will... 176

A Focus on Holism 177

How People Can Attain Positivity... 177

The Actualizing Tendency... 180

Organismic Valuing Process 181

Chapter 26 – The Principle of Utility 184

How Utility Works 184

What About Resources?.. 185

Different from Hedonism 185

Chapter 27 – The Instinct Theory 188

An Example of Instinct 188

Basic Considerations 189

Differing Concepts.. 190

Two Major Problems Surrounding the Instinct Theory...................... 192

Is It Possible for People to Control Instincts? 193

Chapter 28 – Drive-Reduction Theory 195

Understanding the Drive 196

What Is Homeostasis? 196

What Does Drive-Reduction Theory State? 197

Identifying Habits 199

A Learning Point 199

Primary and Secondary Drives 200

Working With Many Drives 202

Any Issues? 202

Will Anyone Ever Be Truly Fulfilled? 203

Chapter 29 – The Social Psychology of Motivation 205

How Is Control Managed? 205

The Key Parts of Any Positive Relationship 206

How Can Social Relationships Improve? 209

Chapter 30 – How Managers Becomes Leaders When Motivating People 212

Focus on Achievements 212

Creativity Is a Must 213

Listen Once In a While 213

Allow for Some Competition 214

Chapter 31 – What Causes People to Impair Motivation? 216

Are People Naturally Evil? 216

A Lack of Empathy 217

A Lack of Oxytocin 218

Too Much Oxytocin 219

Chapter 32 – Positives to Find In Any Motivational Plan 220

Strong Involvement From a Leader 220

What Rewards are Effective? 220

Understand What Motivates Individuals 221

Chapter 33 – A Few Final Points 222

A Need to Be Specific 222

Analyze Fears 222

Intuition Is Vital 223

Keep Working Toward a Goal 223

Do Not Become Overworked 223

Be Prepared 224

The Value of Visualization 224

Allow for Flexibility 225

Be Willing to Dream Big 225

Conclusion 226

Introduction

Businesses are often willing to do anything they can to grow and thrive. They regularly investigate how their employees are working and how they feel about certain situations. It is with this in mind that many psychological considerations come into play. Part of this focuses heavily on motivation, a concept that entails not only people acting in certain ways but also why those people are willing to act that way in the first place. Motivation concerns some factors that cannot be seen or easily identified.

It is common to want to know why people behave as they do and what they can do to possibly change how someone behaves. It is not always easy to identify the forces that are in play to make people act the way they do. If you want to change someone's behavior, it is essential to discover their motivations. When you understand how they live their lives based on certain concepts or ideas, it becomes easier to change their behaviors. The goal of psychology is to have an idea why the human mind acts and thinks the way it does. Every person is unique in his or her own thinking and that person's behaviors can change over time so that the action a person engages in now is different from what that person did long ago.

Many developments have been made in the psychological field to understand how the brain functions. Many of these points relate to the concepts of motivation and productivity.

Motivation is a vital part of the human brain that deserves to be explored in detail. It is through motivation that people engage in certain behaviors. By understanding how motivation works, it can be easier for people to understand what they can do to influence others and to make them feel encouraged to do certain things. This is critical for work environments where it is often a challenge to have people feel confident and motivated about certain processes.

Everyone in the world is motivated by something. Some people are motivated by a need to engage in certain actions. Others might feel a desire to earn a particular reward. There are also times when people are motivated to act by simply avoiding very specific problems or issues that might happen in their lives. It is vital for people in supervisory positions to understand whatever it is that influences and motivates someone to action.

The purpose of this book is to help understand what motivation is and the many theories that make up the science of psychology. A workplace supervisor might use particular theories of motivation that can impact how people in an environment behave.

The concepts listed in this book are useful for workplace managers to use. These concepts could also work in schools and traditional home environments. These concepts provide understanding not only what motivates people to action but also what triggers people into feeling motivated in the first place. An effective supervisor will have the ability to keep someone motivated without causing that original drive to be suppressed.

Motivation includes points relating to cognitive, social, positive, and developmental psychology. Each field is different, but there is always the potential to incorporate the data from the various fields of psychology to use for encouraging motivation in others. The most important point for this guide is that the focus is what can be done to encourage people to be productive. When a person is motivated, it is easier for that person to produce and be active while supporting the requirements of the job at hand, regardless of what that job may be.

The points here focus mainly on what can be done to succeed in the business world, but individual people might also use them in their daily lives.

Author's Request:

If you find this book to be useful, would you be kind enough to leave a positive review on Amazon? I would greatly appreciate it. Thank you.

Chapter 1 – Understanding Motivation and Productivity

When a person in a workplace has a certain job to do, they might feel encouraged to get on that task and act as quickly as possible. However, not all people in the workplace feel the same way. Some people have their own individual reasons why they might want to do a particular chore and others might simply feel a lack of a desire to do it. All of these people are different because they are all being impacted by the concept of motivation in various ways. Some people might feel motivated to get to work, but their sources of motivation will come from different things. Some might be motivated by the potential to make money or to get a promotion. Others might be motivated to work with the fear that they might lose their jobs if they fail to work hard enough. Many people in the same environment might feel a distinct lack of motivation. These include people who feel they are incapable or that the task has no purpose. Others might just feel a sense of malaise or discontent.

Competition might be used as a source of motivation. While many people are motivated to help others and to be friendly, others could be motivated by focusing on their own achievements and treat a situation as a race between themselves and other people.

Whatever the case may be, it is vital to understand how motivation works and what makes it an effective tool in the workplace. It is an intriguing and extensive science in its own right, but it can be easily understood when the many aspects of the concept are reviewed.

A Basic Concept

Motivation is one of the more intriguing points about psychology. Motivation refers to the reasoning behind why a person does any action. It is what causes a person to engage in certain actions and why that person might repeat a particular behavior. Motivation refers to how interested a person is in something and how that person might become committed to a certain action. This may also relate to a person's desire to attain a particular goal.

Those who are not motivated will accomplish nothing. They will not know how to take care of themselves or understand how to make changes in their lives. More importantly, people might have no real direction in life. It would become difficult for a person to do any action if they do not have the motivation to do it.

It is through motivation that people feel a strong desire to do new things or to move forward with what they want to do. Businesses could benefit from understanding how motivation is needed for anyone to do anything. They could use the secrets involved to discover what causes their workers to act in the ways that they do.

An Impact on the Entire Individual

Motivation is critical to understand because it does not just impact one part of an individual's life. It directly influences every aspect of an individual's life including their self-worth. A person who feels motivated will feel confident or thoughtful. A person will know that there is a purpose in life and that hard work has rewards. Someone might work toward making money, becoming healthy, finding love and happiness, and so forth. There are no limits as to what someone might do when they feel motivated.

What Does It Mean to Be Productive?

No matter what one does to find motivation, the end result is always to be productive. It is about productivity through not only getting more things done but also with meeting and maintaining the various requirements in life.

Productivity and motivation are linked to each other. When a person is motivated, that person is capable of completing more tasks and doing more in life. It is easier for tasks in the workplace to be completed so a business eventually becomes more successful and efficient. Meanwhile, all the requirements one has for falling in love, having a family, establishing good relationships with workers and neighbors will be met when one is productive. By being motivated, the productivity that one is capable of tapping into will be fully unlocked. The desire to keep working and to do more with an understanding of why work is valuable will make a true impact on one's life.

A Consistent Process

An intriguing part of motivation is that it does not only occur at one given time. A person has to continue to stay motivated and positive about life in order to succeed and thrive.

More things can be done when someone is confident and continues to be motivated. It is through motivation that people are able to change their lives and consider the things they can do to change themselves. It is vital to stay motivated and positive about life to stay forward-looking and in control of one's life. When a task is appealing and worthwhile, it becomes easier to feel confident and positive while wanting to go forward.

Motivation has to keep on working even when someone meets a certain goal. Although that person might have been motivated to move forward in life and to keep working hard, motivation is still required to go forward. It is vital to keep feeling the same way and to keep on working hard and encouraged to keep on working and do good things for one's life or business.

A Necessity for Health

Motivation and productivity are not only needed for thinking about what can be done in the future. It is also about protecting one's mental health. One of the greatest worries that people often have is to not know what to do in life or what one's purpose might be. Those who do not feel motivated are incapable of functioning well in society or taking care of themselves because they do not know what their priorities are. They cannot move forward to make their lives stronger and more efficient.

Everything that people do in their lives comes from some motives that they have. People who are heavily motivated and know what they want to do are often capable of being more productive and successful. A person who does not have a purpose or does not feel motivated will not have much to do and will not be able to discover ways to get the most out of life. It is through motivation that people are capable of staying focused and capable of doing the things they want to do with their lives.

Many people might not be motivated if they are unable to keep their lives organized or in control. Those who do not know what they want to do with their lives are often at risk of hurting themselves because they do not understand what they can do to make changes. Small problems due to a lack of motivation and organization will only become worse if they do not know how to take care of a situation.

An Indirect Point

One vital aspect of motivation involves how it can be observed. It is not something that people can observe directly. It can be assessed by observing the things that a person is doing in life and how productive that person is. You can observe motivation when you view how people change their lives. For instance, a person might not have been motivated to have a healthy diet in the past. However, motivation might be observed when that person starts to change their dietary routine. Although the reasons why that person is changing their behavior are not visible, they could have had a health scare or might be at risk of a serious health problem. The motivation will clearly be noticeable through the effort and work they are doing to try to change their situation in some way.

Motivation can be seen by the things that a person does at work or at school. A student who works hard in their studies and participates in various after-school programs might be motivated to do one's best. Perhaps that person could be motivated to just simply get a scholarship for college or even an internship in the future.

Goal-Oriented

Motivation and productivity are often associated with goals. That is, people will feel encouraged to work on something if they have goals to achieve. People might have a desire to work toward a goal, but through motivation, more work can be done and the goal to be achieved easier and sooner. The person who completed a certain goal will feel confident and will have the motivation needed to continue if the right goals are established.

The types of goals that people have are varied and diverse. The goals of the individual are not always the same goals as their supervisors'. The ideal situation is when the goals of both are the same and the jobs are completed correctly and on time. An example of this might be something that happens in the workplace. An employee might be motivated to keep on working hard in the hopes of getting a better position in the workplace through a promotion.

Every person will have their own special goals that motivate them. While one person in the workplace might be motivated to work to be given a promotion, another might be motivated to make a business grow or to become more productive. Another employee might just be focused simply on earning money.

The motivation is the psychological influence for a person to want to continue working and doing certain tasks.

Different from Other Concepts

Although motivation and productivity are tied together, there is a distinct attitude that can be noticed within the work a person completes.

Satisfaction

Satisfaction is a concept that focuses on how a person feels positive when certain things are done. Motivation is different from this in that motivation is what leads people toward satisfaction. That is, satisfaction is a vital goal but it can only be attained when a person is motivated.

A person might consider how satisfaction feels and how it can only be attained when certain actions take place. Motivation may help get that person to move toward a state of satisfaction. The key is for a person to realize that by working toward a certain goal or being encouraged to engage in certain actions, they will achieve the end goal of being satisfied and positive about one's work.

Those who do not feel motivated might be incapable of feeling satisfied. They do not fully understand what they should be doing and this keeps them from going forward and getting the most out of their work. When a sensible plan for work is established and a person knows what one wants, it is easier to attain satisfaction.

Naturally, the number of things that can be done in life will relate heavily to one's satisfaction. People often feel satisfied when they notice that they have done more and have been capable of completing more tasks and chores than they intended to do. People know that they have many things on their plates from tasks in their jobs to many points in their personal lives. When someone is motivated, that person's productivity levels increase and they are more likely to accomplish major tasks and eventually become satisfied with the work done.

Inspiration

Although motivation and inspiration may sound rather similar to one another, they are very different. Inspiration focuses on creating a new thought pattern. It entails how a person is going to want to do things in life and focuses more on changing certain attitudes.

A person might have a desire to do something. That is, the person is inspired to feel a need to engage in activities that are more intriguing. There might be an underlying factor that might cause someone to want to do things. However, it is through motivation that propels someone to take action.

People have to be motivated to want to keep working and do things in their lives.

A person might be inspired to do something by another person in a workplace or maybe by a family member. The motivation that one has could come from an inspiration to be like someone else. One ideal example is if a person sees a number of slim models and would become inspired to lose weight to look more like one of those models. The motivation is the thought process for that person to actually change their behavior or take action.

Having a sense of inspiration might help a person to become motivated. The inspiration is not necessarily going to cause that person to actually be motivated in the first place. It takes extra effort to help a person learn how to stay inspired and ready to work and act. The inspiration in question has to be positive and reflective of the needs that someone has in life. By establishing a strong relationship with an inspiration, it becomes easier for a person to stay focused. When that inspiration is lost or a person begins to have second thoughts about it, it becomes difficult to stay motivated and focused.

Manipulation

Manipulation is often seen as a more difficult part of psychology that is a challenge. This happens when someone feels or is made to feel that they have to work in certain ways. A person might be manipulated so that he or she will want to engage in certain actions. Manipulation happens when someone uses a force of some kind without the subject's permission or knowledge. People who manipulate others will do what they can to make people do things they would not ordinarily do on their own. Even though the manipulator might have the best of intentions and wants people to be productive and active, this is not always going to be the right kind of action for people to engage in. It could be ethically wrong because it keeps people from being able to make their own decisions and to be inspired to stay productive.

Motivation is a gentle aspect of psychology. It is not forcing people to take certain actions. Rather, it encourages people to specific actions. The people who are motivated can choose their own methods for going forward and to do better things in their lives. This may cause people to be more productive because they will be motivated by things or ideas that they feel comfortable with. They are not at risk of being harmed or impacted by anything negative.

One point that will be discussed later in this guide is the art of incentive motivation. This relates to encouraging people to engage in certain actions by offering rewards. This is gentler than manipulation because it does not involve forcing someone into an action. It is rather about simply letting someone know that there is a good reward available for doing something.

The Overall Goal of Motivation

The main point about motivation is that it is all about finding a way to make a person feel satisfied with something. It is getting a person to feel as though his or her efforts in the workplace or in school among other places are worthwhile and that a person will reap some benefit. By allowing a person to feel motivated, it becomes easier for a business to thrive and move forward. People who are motivated are capable of doing extra in the workplace. They know that there is something on the other end for them when they are working on a project. It is vital for anyone in the workplace to be aware of their contribution and that it is appreciated.

This also helps a person experience a sense of purpose. It is often difficult for people to feel happy about their lives if they do not see a purpose for whatever it is they are doing. By establishing a purpose, it becomes easier for someone to stay motivated and to want to keep moving forward.

Those who are not motivated will not understand why they are working or realize the benefits of their work. The questions they have about why they are doing certain things and what they have to offer within the workplace will make it more difficult for a person to want to keep working as they do not see the reasons for working.

The overall point about motivation is that it is something that can be rather intriguing and unique. The many things that can happen when motivation and productivity are considered are all worth exploring.

Chapter 2 – Why Is Motivation so Important?

To be productive in life is vital, but to get there, a person has to be appropriately motivated. There needs to be a clear sense of control and vision for one's life that makes it easier for a person to want to continue working on certain tasks.

It is through motivation that people are capable of going forward in their lives to do whatever they can in life. With motivation, businesses are capable of completing their many tasks while students at schools will finish their assignments and get the best grades possible. Without motivation, people will not think about what they want to do or how they want to change or improve their lives.

Motivation is also needed to help people understand what they can do and how they will stay in control. People who are motivated will have a good idea of what they might do in their lives and how they will work. As this chapter will explain, there are many aspects of motivation that have to be explored to understand why it is so critical for people to see how this can work in general.

Managing Resources Well

A vital point about motivation is that it encourages people to think about how they will manage their resources appropriately. It is through motivation that people will consider those resources and get ready to move ahead in life. These resources often entail money to afford to work on certain tasks, physical resources from other people or materials, and even one's personal thoughts and values. Motivation makes it easier for people to take all those resources and to turn them into actual things that might be valuable to them or others. People might realize that certain resources are more vital and more important than others. This knowledge will change someone's attitudes and will either limit one's goals or expand them.

Added Productivity

The productivity that comes with being motivated may be the most popular benefit of motivation that people look for. It is often frustrating to go through life and notice that one has not done all that much of anything due to a lack of motivation. A workplace where people are encouraged to get to work and feel a strong desire for doing so will not only be a happier and more inviting place but also a spot where people will want to stay focused and active.

Workplaces are often saddled with people who might not feel motivated. When people are not motivated, it becomes harder for them to think about what they can do with the resources they have been provided. They might feel that they cannot actually do much with what they are given. They are only showing up to work because they either want to be paid or it is just a routine that is hard to break. Others may begin to question what they are encountering in their lives. They might assume that certain things are worth hardly anything and that they don't even know what they are doing or why.

Motivation encourages people to think about what they can do and allows them to look at the resources they are given and the skills they have. By using motivation, it becomes easier for people to want to keep working and to move forward with their lives. They will want to actively do more for their employers and think more about how they can make work easier and be more productive. People will actually want to come to work.

A business could benefit from knowing how to motivate people in order to reduce operating costs. As a business reduces its costs, it becomes easier for that business to grow and thrive. Properly motivated, the workers in the workplace will be productive and will do more each day, thus improving efficiency. This is a necessity for success.

Establish Strong Relationships

People develop better relationships when they are motivated. They feel more comfortable when working on certain projects because they know what to do and they are getting some kind of help from others close to them. This also helps people realize they are not alone when trying to complete tasks and stay productive.

The overall relationship someone has with one's employer might be stronger. The employee is more apt to become much more productive thanks to that sense of encouragement and a newfound desire to keep working hard.

Sometimes the use of promotional opportunities or special rewards might help build strong relationships. It is all about letting people feel confident in their abilities and what they are accomplishing together.

A Sense of Stability

Motivation encourages a better sense of stability in the workplace. When everyone in the workplace is motivated and encouraged to be productive, it becomes easier for the workplace to stay intact. People will feel satisfied with their jobs and will want to continue to work with other people in their areas. This helps create a comfortable environment where everyone involved will feel excited about the work that they are doing. When a business knows what motivates its workers and how people might be inspired to do more, the business benefits. Everyone will get along and establishes a more positive mindset in the workplace.

When there is no stability, there is a sense of fear. People will not be certain as to what they will be doing in the future nor do they feel that they have very many opportunities to advance. The added stress and fear of uncertainties and questions about the future make it more difficult for people to want to work hard.

A Need to Attain Goals

It takes a great amount of emotional and mental effort for a person to reach a certain goal. This is especially true if a person is struggling to complete certain tasks. A person might need to have or be given a strong sense of motivation to help move toward a goal.

For instance, a person might have to work on an extensive database project in a workplace. That project might be very lengthy and could take weeks or months to complete. Over time, it becomes easy for a person to feel a lack of motivation. This is perhaps because the person is struggling to complete the entire project. It could become repetitive after a while and cause the person to lose motivation.

A person who is appropriately motivated will feel confident and will want to continue with the project at hand. They will feel positive about the end result or even encouraged to work just to help the business. Sometimes that person might be motivated by the potential of receiving extra money or a promotion. The type of motivation used can vary, but it is all about prompting someone to realize that there needs to be an effort in place to work hard and move forward with a task.

A Sense of Esteem

Another part of what makes motivation important is that it is vital to give people self-esteem. People are often willing to work hard if they feel that they are appreciated. Those who feel confident are more likely to stay motivated. Those who are motivated will feel satisfied and may not need encouragement from others. Good self-esteem ensures that someone will be more productive while on the job.

Motivation is essential in business. A business that has employed many motivated people will thrive and be more successful thanks to the hard work people are willing to do.

Chapter 3 – A Basic Cycle

People are motivated by many things, but there is a simple equation that can be used to understand the basics of motivation and productivity. Every act of motivation is based on a cycle, which is vital for psychological considerations in that it looks into what causes people to act.

Four Vital Steps

There are four steps that make up a basic motivational cycle. These are to be followed in the appropriate order for the entire process to be accomplished appropriately. The cycle can also be repeated many times as necessary:

1. Need

Any action is influenced by a certain need. It could be a basic need one has for survival or just something that a person wants. It might also come from a timing demand, such as having to finish a task within a certain time. The need could be a desire for money or a need to be with other people.

The need is often in response to an imbalance in the mind or body. The person will feel a need to finish a certain task based on what they might have done in the past. The rest of the cycle is devoted to satisfying that need to create a better balance.

2. Drive

The drive follows need: the greater the need, the greater the drive. Certain actions to complete the task at hand or to satisfy one's need are to be developed and then implemented at this juncture. The drive might cause a sense of tension, but it will allow a person to keep on working and to move forward.

For instance, a person might have the drive to work by doing certain things in the workplace or in school to get to the end goal. The tension involved might come from a person being uncertain at the start or even from disagreements with others, but the overall goal is to establish an attitude that is consistent and creates the power to move forward.

3. Incentive

As the drive is utilized to satisfy the need, an incentive is needed. This is a vital part of the motivational process to influence people. When a person knows that there is an incentive attached to a performance, that person will want to continue working. This might come from a need to get a good grade, to earn extra money, or to receive some benefit personally from the work done. The incentive creates a purpose for the work done, whether it is receiving money or just the satisfaction of a job well done, there has to be some reward at the end of the road.

4. Goal

After all the hard work and the overall motivation that comes from an incentive or just a need to satisfy a need, the goal needs to be attained. The person will have collected the incentive for reaching the goal and the cycle can begin again.

The goal does not always have to be something positive. It could also have a negative connotation in some cases. For instance, a person might have a goal to avoid certain stimuli or other threats that might influence one's work.

The cycle is simple and easy to understand. The general goal is to fully understand how certain concepts might work in any given case.

A Simple Example

To get an idea of how the cycle works, here is an example. Let's say that a student in high school is hoping to get a college scholarship. To do so, she would have to do very well on a certain exam. She has a need at this point to want to attain a certain score on that exam. She would have an imbalance in her mind as she is overly concerned about trying to get that scholarship. This would lead her toward determining what she can do to be successful and to get the support she needs.

That imbalance occurs as she has a major task that needs to be done soon. By completing the task, that imbalance will be resolved and she can get back to the status quo or some state of homeostasis that she had before.

She will then have the drive to reach that goal of succeeding in her test. She will look for ways to do so, whether it is studying hard or organizing her practices for the test. Her effort is all about being active and ready to do what is possible to satisfy that need.

The incentive will then be established based on what she feels will be good enough for her. The incentive in her case might be getting that scholarship. The incentive, in this case, is the motivation as she will feel encouraged to keep working hard and to do what she can to actually get the scholarship funds that she is hoping for.

The final point is the goal. The student's goal is to achieve a certain grade on her test. She will succeed in getting to that goal when she passes the test with the marks necessary to attain the scholarship she wants. The goal is the ultimate end result gained by her motivation to succeed.

By reviewing the cycle, it helps to understand the many theories of the act of motivation. This also helps with identifying the needs that a person holds and how they can be resolved.

This cycle is something that can be noticed in practically every aspect of motivation. It can work even when a specific theory is introduced. Anyone who observes somebody in action will have to decide how such concepts might be orchestrated.

Chapter 4 – The Three Key Parts of Motivation

Everyone is motivated in their own particular ways. It is through motivation that the human mind activates the body to perform. When someone has the motivation, they will find it easier to perform tasks and complete jobs. This is vital for a person to have a strong sense of control over what can be done in any situation. When a person does not feel motivated, it becomes difficult to accomplish anything.

Anyone could have a goal in life. A person might have a desire to finish a certain work project before a specific time. A person could have a need to do something like buy a home or find a new job or even lose weight. Sometimes those goals might be nothing more than thoughts because those people were not motivated to take action.

The art of motivation is complicated, but it can be boiled down to three vital parts. These are aspects of motivation that directly influence how people think and what they might do when trying to move forward. When these are used, it is easy for the natural cycle of motivation to start working.

The three parts of motivation focus extensively on the following points:

1. Activating a strong desire to go forward

2. Being concentrated with enough intensity to keep going forward

3. Being persistent in staying motivated toward a goal even when certain problems get in the way

This chapter focuses on all three of these points. They relate to both getting ready to be motivated and understanding what has to be done to stay motivated and upbeat about anything that you may wish to do.

Activation

Every action has to be initiated. There exists a period of activation where someone is going to go forward and do something. If a person is not activated, it becomes harder for that person to go far. There is always going to be a chance that a problem might develop.

To get someone to be motivated and ready to be productive takes a trigger event or some other stimuli to get that person to act. This varies with each person, but it is the key to giving someone the ability to move ahead in life.

The process of activation is what causes a person to engage in a certain behavior. In most cases, there is a goal that someone might have. Activation can happen because other people are doing something or because friends and family want something to happen. In other cases, it may come from a perceived threat of a negative issue to occur for not taking action. Whatever the threat or worry might be, there lies a need for someone to work hard and want to take action. A good example is when a person might have a desire to join the football team at their high school. He might make a conscious decision to try out for that team. When he starts that behavior, he is activated.

This is what starts the cycle of motivation. Someone notices that a certain action is required and then decides to do it. The goal is to decide what action is needed.

Intensity

The intensity refers to the amount of effort placed on a particular move. A person will be motivated by certain intensity depending on the perceived need.

In the football example, the student wants to join the team by working hard to be given a roster spot. He is working on this by engaging in regular activities like lifting weights, running laps around a track and so forth. He is trying to get his body in shape and to become not only stronger but also capable of handling some of the quick moves that a person needs to do to prove he is capable of joining the team. His intensity is important as he is focusing on trying to move forward and succeed. A person who is more intense in one's efforts is more likely to go further and attain their goal.

The best way to consider intensity is to see it as a drive. When the intensity is high, the drive is greater. When that drive is nonexistent, it is easy for that person to forget about what the motivation was in the first place. The spark that triggered the activation will soon die.

Persistence

Persistence is a part of the motivation that allows for consistently moving toward a certain action. There might be a series of obstacles in the way, but a person who is motivated will be persistent and not give up.

After a person has activated a goal and is motivated, that person will work hard to keep on moving forward. It is through persistence that a person can achieve their goal. Sometimes problems might interfere and those problems will be overcome with persistence. For example, the high school student might notice that there are many people at the same school who also want to get on the football team. Some of them might be very interested in the particular positions that he wants to play. Therefore, he would have to keep on thinking about what he can do to get on the team and how he can make his skills stand out. When he is persistent and keeps on focusing on his goal of making the team, he is more likely to actually make it.

Persistence does require a greater amount of effort for one to succeed. For instance, a student might have to think about employing more exercise time or cutting other activities to practice harder to make the football team. That investment in time and effort can pay off as it becomes easier to work toward that ultimate goal. As that goal is attained, the student will feel positive about his efforts.

There might also be cases where certain obstacles get in the way to make it even harder to sustain persistence. The student might get injured and would be unable to continue his efforts to get on the team, for instance. The persistence the student has would help him to move through the injury and to recover so that he can continue his effort in trying to get on that team.

A certain behavior will be activated while that person is intense about reaching his goal. The persistence will be extensive and will focus on what the student can do to move forward and keep on trying to succeed despite the obstacles in his way.

Chapter 5 – Managing Both Desires

A with many other mental concepts, motivation comes from within. Although one person might tell a second that something has to be done or that certain actions should be followed, it is up to that second person to feel encouraged and motivated to do it.

Motivation is a practice that occurs from two vital desires in the human mind. The first is the fundamental needs that a person has and the other is the ego and how it drives a person to feel differently about the self.

Fundamental Desires

Motivation often supports fundamental needs that people have. These include the things that people need to survive and feel protected, such as the need for food, shelter, clothing, and anything else one cannot survive without.

These are among the more threatening points that cause people to be productive. Someone who has food, shelter, and clothing can be motivated to work, but the motivation becomes even greater when any of those needs are missing. The threats that occur when not getting the things that one needs for life are often significant. The immediate sense of threat and panic will make it harder for that person to be active and ready to take action.

Money is one of the more common fundamental desires that might be part of the motivational process. In today's society, any of the fundamental needs that people have cannot be met unless they have enough money. By getting enough money, it is easier for people to attain what they want. Motivation might be influenced by the basic desire to have money.

Sometimes the fundamental desires can become more significant. For instance, a person might be in a condition where he is trying to pay his monthly rent for an apartment and is struggling to actually have the money he needs. He may then be motivated to work more hours at his job or to try to find a better job that pays more. When the mind contemplates the needs one has above all else, it becomes easier for one to move forward with a plan to work harder to satisfy that need.

More importantly, this is all about survival. People are often at their most vulnerable when they are concerned about their survival. By managing one's fundamental needs, the fears of survival are alleviated and life becomes less concerning and worrisome.

The key to these desires is that they are the ones that will be felt first. Certain ego-based desires might start to manifest themselves and become more valuable. This is where the next part of the motivation comes into play.

Ego-Based Desires

The human ego is one's idea of self-importance. The ego determines what someone might think about one's life and how well that person feels.

Ego-based desires occur only after the fundamental needs are met. At this point, a person will have a sense of comfort in one's life and will be ready to try and move forward in some way.

While someone might have satisfied all their fundamentals needs, they might want to move forward even more and work toward managing some of the other desires that he or she has.

The ego can be triggered by many things:

- People might recognize someone for doing something positive. This includes awarding someone a prize or other special recognition for being above one's peers in the workplace.

- The ego can be enhanced when a person is regularly contacted or supported by others. At this point, the person will feel that he or she is appreciated by others.

- The ego might be triggered by a desire to complete a certain task before anyone else.

The ego might cause a person to feel motivated. This occurs as the person might feel a desire to be recognized or to be appreciated by others. This could be interpreted as being useful for someone's image in that they are more likely to be recognized as being someone who understands his or her role in a certain environment.

An example of ego-based motivation could be just trying to stand out. For instance, there might be twenty different people working in an office who are vying to attain a special annual honor for work done. Mr. X and Mrs. Y, two workers at the building, might feel motivated by not only being recognized but also by competing with one another. Mr. X might want to finish more tasks than everyone else, and Mrs. Y might feel a need to be more punctual and accurate by finishing her work in a more detailed fashion.

The two would be motivated to work in their own ways, but they will have the same end goal. They want to be productive and capable of showing that they can do a job better than their peers. It is all about their ability to be productive and efficient. Sometimes the rewards that come with a job well done can trigger positive feelings, which will boost the ego.

Chapter 6 – Maslow's Theory of Needs and Wants

It is vital to look at the many individual theories that directly influence motivation at this point. Although motivation is necessary to understand, there are many points relating to the concept that deserves to be explored. One particular aspect of motivation to discuss is the case of Maslow's theory of needs and wants.

This concept is often seen as a basic part of the motivation. It focuses on some of the basic requirements that people have in their lives and looks at how those needs change over time. It can be used as a base concept for how to identify what makes people act in the ways that they do.

This theory identifies an extensive variety of concepts and ideas. The needs that people have in their lives are diverse and are not only things for survival but also things for advancement.

Motivation is often influenced by the needs and wants that people have and make decisions about what they want and how to use assets they find to their advantage. The goal is to find a way to resolve the many needs that one has while also satisfying their wants. The greatest concern about needs and wants is that they influence how well a person is motivated. When a person's needs are all met, it is often difficult for that person to feel a desire to move to satisfy their wants. The needs are essentially the bare minimum that person requires out of life. To satisfy a person's wants require an extra bit of work.

The concept of needs and wants and how they relate to motivation was developed by Abraham Maslow. The American psychologist developed a simple pyramid that focuses on understanding how people need certain things and how that can satisfy the many wants that a person has.

The pyramid that Maslow created focuses on five needs:

1. Physiological

2. Safety

3. Love

4. Esteem

5. Self-Actualization

The basic point that Maslow uses is a mix of basic and complex needs. A person will have their basic needs met first. Then, the person can begin to satisfy the more detailed or complicated needs.

Physiological

Maslow's pyramid starts with a series of basic physiological needs.

First, a person might have a need for security. This includes having the proper shelter needed for life. When a person has a secure home that one can pay for and own and will not be at risk of being removed from, it is easier for that person to feel confident. People are motivated to arrange for their housing and safety needs so that they are not at risk of finding themselves in places where they are not comfortable.

Second, a person has physical needs. These basic needs concentrate on the ability of a person to feel comfortable with one's body and to stay physically protected. These needs are the desires to eat and sleep among other basics. Enough food, water, and space for sleeping are required to keep the body protected. When this need is not fulfilled, a person will feel threatened. This is critical for motivation as many people are motivated to eat, sleep, and do other basic things because they know they would be at risk of harm if they do not engage in behaviors relating to those needs.

One's health is also important to recognize here. When a person is healthy, this physiological need is met. The body is not at risk of harm and will provide that person with the ability to keep on doing the things they want to do. Sex is often seen as the most basic need that people have, although it is typically seen as an optional activity. When people engage in sex, they feel secure about their bodies. They start to feel that there is nothing that they cannot do in their lives.

The basic needs a person has are considered deficiency needs. When someone does not have these needs met, a deficiency is felt. The person might feel inferior to others because they are not getting the support or resources to stay happy and in control. It is through hard work and effort that people aim to meet these needs.

Fear is also a common motivator. A person who cannot get the things needed to handle basic requirements for a living will be afraid that things will only become worse. There might be general fears of being unable to help other people or being unable to stay happy.

People are often more likely to be productive at this stage in the pyramid. This is the point where people will know that their lives need to be enhanced and supported. By working to satisfy the needs one has, a person will feel safe.

Safety

As a person grows and feels confident with the basics needs met, it becomes easier for that person to feel safe and relaxed. As a result, the person will start to satisfy some other needs. These needs focus on personal growth to become positive and confident.

The safety needs are focused on keeping one's physiological needs sustained. These needs will cause people be more productive. The threats that a person might encounter in their life could be significant. These include threats relating to one's health and an ability to actually move forward and get the money needed for keeping one's life intact. Being able to handle all the safety needs is a necessity for life, thus making it easier for a person to stay productive and active.

Six points regarding safety needs:

1. Long-term health

Although one's immediate health is critical, the long-term health is even more important. People are often motivated to keep their health in check so they can live longer and avoid many significant expenses relating to medical issues. It is because of this that many people are motivated to find health insurance.

2. Employment

The physiological needs that someone has cannot be met unless one has a job. Employment is a need that focuses on being able to pay their debts. Having a job also makes a person feel more comfortable knowing that there is going to be some way for that person to have the money needed to pay for what they need.

A person might be motivated to keep working in a job to not only continue to have it but to also possibly move forward and have a better potential for earning even more money.

3. Resources

A person requires resources for life like water sources, funds from a bank account and a place where people can work. A person who has enough resources will feel comfortable and ready to move on to the next part of the pyramid. It is even more important for that person has a consistent flow of resources. When the flow is steady, it becomes easier for a person to feel secure. That person may even be motivated to ensure that those resources will continue to flow and that there will be no risk of losing those resources at any time in the future.

4. Morality

People are motivated to live by their own moral codes. When someone feels that their basic needs have been met, that person can start to live by a code of behavior. Those who do not have the physiological needs they require are often motivated to engage in harmful behaviors that might be against a moral code simply because they just want to be on the same playing field as everyone else.

5. Family

Those who can handle the most basic requirements in their lives are capable of having families. People are often motivated to have stronger families and to be able to support larger families. A family could consist of not only a spouse and children but also parents or siblings and other key family members and that a personal connection is established.

6. Property

It is one thing for a person to have a good home. It is another to actually have a property one can feel comfortable with. The property need focuses on how a person is able to hold onto a space for living without feeling threatened.

A person who is living in an apartment might feel comfortable, but that person might be motivated to own a home. That home will allow the person to have a permanent place in which to reside.

By meeting these six safety needs, a person will feel positive about what one is doing with life. It is about not only having the basics but also feeling as though those basics are not going to be taken away or changed easily.

Love

The motivational process includes social and personal points as to how certain relationships are established. Love is a vital psychological need. People are motivated to fall in love after they have their basic needs taken care of and they are relatively secure in their circumstances and they feel the need to move forward with finding a personal relationship.

Not all people will feel motivated to find love exactly the same way. Some people might just want to be close to another. A good love relationship will include three vital points for success. A person does not have to go through all three of them, but the ones who do will feel the most self-realized and confident in their lives:

1. Friendship

A person might start by simply having a good friendship with someone to confide in. The friendship may eventually develop to become more physically closer in time.

This is the most basic part of this section of the pyramid. A person does not have to go beyond the friendship part. The key is just having some support to find encouragement to stay productive and happy. There is always the chance for that relationship to blossom and become stronger and more intimate, which leads to the next point.

2. Intimacy

What starts out as a friendship may develop into intimacy and may lead to sex. The intimacy should eventually lead to a more secure link between the two people. In some cases, it might lead to marriage if those two people are confident in one another and willing to be committed to each other.

Intimacy is often needed to ensure that two people are confident in each other. When the two people involved know each other both emotionally and physically, a sense of confidence and positivity will come about over time. The positive feelings that two people hold will give each other the feeling that a relationship is real and will last over time. This leads to confidence in the arrangement and will move toward having larger long-term goals.

3. Family

If the relationship feels secure, it will move on to marriage and then to starting a family. This is a need that people are motivated to have. By having a good love relationship, it becomes easier for the people involved to feel positive. The motivation that one has at this juncture will be all about having a better personal life where the support that one gets is paramount to success and happiness. More importantly, a person will feel productive thanks to the knowledge that there is someone with whom to share responsibilities and give support.

Esteem

The fourth need that a person has is having a strong sense of esteem. Those who can attain this part of Maslow's pyramid will feel confident and know they have done what they want to do with their lives. Those who have self-esteem have a sense of productivity and get the most out of the work one wants to complete. This requires extra effort for success and it will become easier for someone to feel happy about their life.

After a person is capable of getting a steady job, enjoying a good relationship, having a healthy routine and has plenty of people for support, it becomes easy for that person to be motivated toward finding ways to achieve more. Part of this involves finding confidence. When the person is motivated, the other needs that one had earlier will be interpreted as having been met. The odds of that person moving down the pyramid will be extremely minimal at this juncture. This all comes amid a basic feeling of desire and care for one's future and ability to do more with it in general.

Struggles Being Motivated

Although the esteem part of the pyramid is vital, it is often difficult for people to feel motivated enough to actually get through this part of the pyramid and finally reach the top. The problem many people have is that they feel they already have everything that they need to be comfortable with their lives.

However, they might not be fully aware of how there are many other things they could do.

There might be cases where a person is no longer productive after reaching a certain part of the pyramid. That person might think that everything is fine thanks to the security one has or the satisfying relationship that one has. The best way to feel motivated when one is comfortable is finding a way to gain self-actualization, which leads to the final part of the pyramid.

Self-Actualization

The final goal for anyone to attain is self-actualization. It is here that a person will feel comfortable and completely satisfied with their life. When a person reaches self-actualization, many positives can happen:

1. That person might feel creative and have unique and fun ideas for life. At this point, the person will feel positive about where they are going and will want to help others. The overall welfare of humanity is more important to a self-actualized person than their own welfare.

2. The person feels spontaneous with the knowledge that there are no limits or restrictions as to what one can do in life.

3. Problem-solving focuses on how a person might be capable of resolving various issues. That person is never going to be self-centered.

4. A person will feel positive about life and might have a good sense of humor even when facing obstacles.

5. Someone would be willing to accept facts. That person will not be afraid of what others think.

6. The moral or ethical rules for a person who attains self-actualization will be specific and distinct.

Self-actualization occurs when a person feels competent and secure that they can handle any problem that might happen in life. It is here that one's maximum potential can finally be reached. A person will stay productive and active and never have to worry or be afraid of what might happen because they are secure.

The important point about this aspect is that it could take a while for someone to attain this level. It could take years before anyone reaches a state of self-actualization. The entire pyramid has to be conquered from top to bottom even if it takes a long time to do so. The proper foundations are set in one's life before self-actualization can occur.

Does This Have to Work in Order?

When Maslow produced this theory of motivation, he made it with the intention of people following a particular order. He organized it based on what he felt was important for people to follow.

One criticism that many people have about this theory of motivation is that the order that Maslow described does not always have to be followed exactly. Many argue that there is no reason why the lowest needs always have to be resolved before the higher needs can be fulfilled. For instance, people in poor parts of the world might still be able to find love and feel positive about their lives even if they do not have the money or shelter they need.

The concept might vary based on where one lives and how well certain philosophies are established. Every person is going to take the concepts listed here very differently, but they are all going to have to be attained at some point or another if the pyramid is actually to be supported.

This is essentially the opposite of the ERG theory, a point that will be covered later in this guide. The ERG theory allows people to go from one part of the pyramid to another. Maslow simply focuses on a strict order for his pyramid with the belief that some values are more important than others and that it would be impossible to handle certain needs before others are actually met.

How Businesses Can Use the Pyramid

The concepts introduced in the Maslow pyramid can be used by businesses to help identify how far people are going in their lives and what is influencing them. By talking with individual employees in the workplace about their lives, it becomes apparent where on the pyramid a person might be.

Questionnaires may be developed and sent out to employees to ask them about their lives. People might talk about how they are managing their needs as well as the desires they hold. It might be easier for a business to decide who is ripe for advancement based on where they are on the pyramid.

The results of each questionnaire may also help understand how motivated people might be to handle certain tasks in the workplace. Results can include a review of how well a person feels about the situations within the workplace. Employers can eventually target individual workers with different strategies to get them motivated. This is all about identifying the requirements and demands that people have for their lives and how they can be influenced in a positive way.

Businesses can also review how productive and proficient people are in the workplace. People can be reviewed based on how they perform their tasks or their proficiency. Businesses can identify what motivation is involved with the people who are working well. They could be the most motivated, but whether or not those people are at the peak of the pyramid might be unclear.

The Value of Meta motivation

The general goal for anyone according to Maslow's pyramid is to attain a sense of self-actualization. It is at this point that a person will feel fully accomplished.

The greatest concern for those who have reached the peak of Maslow's pyramid is enough and they might no longer feel fully motivated. The truth is that a person must continue to feel motivated if that someone is going to stay at the peak of the pyramid.

Continued motivation is required to allow a person who has it all to keep putting in a strong effort and moves forward with a better attitude for work helps maintain positive results.

Maslow addresses this through a concept known as meta motivation. This is a concept where the human mind is capable of moving forward to be more inventive and thoughtful. Maslow has argued that when a person reaches the top of his pyramid, that person may feel no need to be motivated. Maslow encourages the development of meta motivation, which encourages a person to explore additional needs that they might have.

For Maslow, people who follow meta motivation are capable of being themselves while staying true to their values. They can become spontaneous and likely to want to do things in their lives without worrying about other issues getting in the way. The odds of a person falling further down the pyramid and having to do things all over again would be minimal at this juncture.

Metaneeds

A part of meta motivation involves the use of metaneeds. These are the attributes of living that people can look to follow when they have attained the self-actualization. Those who move forward with their metaneeds are more likely to feel positive and confident in everything they are doing.

Metaneeds come in many forms to help with continuing the movement of self-actualization and feeling confident in one's ability to do things and go far in life. The metaneeds that Maslow has described are:

1. Wholeness – A need to feel a sense of unity and control in life.

2. Perfection – A sense of harmony where there are no obstacles.

3. Completion – A feeling that the path to the top is completed and finished.

4. Justice – Being fair to other people.

5. Richness – Being detailed and complex.

6. Simplicity – Understanding the general essence of what one wants to do with life.

7. Liveliness – The ability to do anything at any moment in time.

8. Beauty – Feeling good about how one looks and feels.

9. Goodness – Feeling benevolent and positive toward other people.

10. Uniqueness – A sense of being an individual who is different from everyone else.

11. Playfulness – Knowing that life is easy and that there is nothing to be worried about.

12. Truth – Recognizing the reality of the world and being positive about what is happening.

13. Autonomy – Being self-sufficient without having to be overly reliant on other people.

14. Meaningfulness – Knowing that one has a value and is capable of doing anything valuable or helpful to others.

A person could attain self-actualization by having a good sense of understanding about what attributes one wants to have. When meta motivation is used, it becomes easier for a person to become stronger.

Sometimes it might be difficult to get it to the place where a person can move forward through meta motivation. The next chapter focuses on what can be done to assist people to make it through meta motivation even as the Jonah Complex is being felt.

Chapter 7 – The Jonah Complex (A Fear of Success)

Everyone in the workplace will do what they can to try to succeed. They will want to perform to their best potential and will be motivated by others to feel positive about their work. When they work to their best potential, it becomes easier for them to move ahead in their lives and to truly succeed. Sometimes a person may be too afraid to go any further to do more in life.

As appealing as self-actualization may be, there is one prominent emotional struggle that often makes it hard for some people to attain this level of success. This is known as the Jonah Complex and it is an aspect of living that makes it harder for people to go further. It is another part of the hierarchy of needs that was developed by Maslow and is relevant to working toward getting people to feel motivated as they attain the ultimate point of meta motivation.

The Jonah Complex is when a person is afraid to do anything more in the future and is not willing to accomplish anything else. That person might be talented, but not motivated to go further. This is a significant problem in many workplace settings because it keeps people from being capable of helping their fellow workers. People might have the skills needed to help others and to make a business grow while also helping those skilled people to move further and earn more money.

This issue could keep a business from growing because its most talented workers are not able to offer the services that they should be able to provide. The best way to describe the Jonah Complex is that it is a fear of success. When a business understands what can be done to counter the Jonah Complex, it can become more profitable.

Background

The Jonah Complex takes its name from the story of Jonah in the Hebrew Bible. The prophet had escaped his destiny to prophesize the full destruction of Nineveh. It is one of the more familiar stories that people know from the book as it tells of Jonah risking his life to avoid the destiny that he was supposed to have.

To Maslow, the Jonah Complex refers to how a person might feel a desire to ignore and refuse some responsibilities. These include duties that a person has due to fate or just luck. This means that a person is trying to avoid one's destiny just as Jonah tried to do in the Bible.

The main problem with the Jonah Complex is that it is the time when a person might feel afraid to do something and try to avoid the duties and responsibilities that one should hold. In short, a person fears one's own greatness, thus keeping that person from feeling motivated to attain self-actualization.

This part of motivation often keeps businesses from moving forward. At the same time, it may also be a sign of anxiety within a person. The fear of what can happen is a clear concern that could easily influence what a person can do in the workplace and change a person's attitude.

Common Signs

There are many ways a person might begin to develop a fear of success or get embroiled in the Jonah Complex. Many of these signs show that a person wants to take that next step but is not able to actually do it for many reasons:

1. That person might feel guilty about the success one has had.

A lack of motivation often comes from guilt. A person who is successful might be upset because they are experiencing a lot of success but others in their family or workplace are not having the same levels of success. Sometimes people believe they are being humble and that they should not worry about what they are feeling. In reality, this is actually going to do more to hurt a person or the business and keep it from growing.

The guilt that someone feels might be because they believe others are going to be upset because they are not doing as well. However, in reality, those who are not as successful will more than likely feel admiration. It is the fear of being judged or of letting other people down that might hinder someone's desire to move ahead.

2. A person might not want to tell other people about their accomplishments.

This is another sign of a person trying to act humble. A person who does this might think he or she is not trying to be too high above others, but at this point, that person's skills are not being used. It becomes hard for that person to offer encouragement to others.

In some cases, a person might feel as though their accomplishments are insignificant and there is no reason for attention. In some cases, a person might become worried about how those accomplishments are interpreted by others. That person might be afraid of being ostracized.

The worst part about this issue is that it is not always logical. People appreciate and are often willing to support someone who is accomplished.

3. Someone might try to delay big projects.

For instance, a worker might want to avoid preparing for a huge design project for an architectural firm. She might think that she could fail because the task would bring a lot of attention toward her. The fear she has is that she could be recognized for the work she does. While it's true that she could fear being blamed for a failure, in most cases a person who is stuck in the Jonah Complex might feel a fear of being heralded for one's work. This is another self-centered attitude that makes it harder for a person to be treated seriously or to be positive.

The general concern is that a person is too anxious about what might happen. The fear of not doing well with something new is a problem that many people obsess over. This keeps them from feeling motivated and makes them feel they would rather avoid a task that appears too large and stay where one is already comfortable.

Those who might depend on such large projects will be impacted the most. People might need to have certain tasks finished first above all. When one person holds up one of these tasks, it becomes hard for the task itself to be fully completed. Other people will suffer because of one person is struggling with the Jonah Complex, thus making it all the more important to review and to prevent this from happening.

4. Certain projects might be compromised or altered intentionally.

The main reason why a person alters projects or other tasks is to avoid problems from happening. The person perceives that there are particular problems that might get in the way and make life harder. In reality, that person is actually causing more hurt to themselves.

Even though a person might feel that problems might occur, often there is no evidence that such issues will actually happen. What is even worse is that person might try to convince others that those problems will happen without evidence.

5. A person could feel that he or she does not deserve the success.

Even with all the work that went into becoming successful, a person might begin to feel that there is no reason why they are in a positive position. There might be a feeling that he or she is not actually doing something worthwhile and is only going to be a burden to others because of that success. This is the Jonah Complex at work. The person might have felt as though they were incapable but accomplished things because of luck. That person might be underestimating their skills or strengths, thus leading to a strong sense of uncertainty over what they can do in life.

Many people who are successful do indeed deserve it because they have put in the effort to have success. Those who feel otherwise might assume that they are going to be judged by their background and past accomplishments.

6. There is a worry that any success will be impossible to sustain.

While there is always a potential for some forms of success to continue, it might be hard for some to actually maintain the success they have. They might fear that they will be under pressure and stress to do more and fail at some point.

These signs are relatively easy to spot in most people in the workplace. They might have second thoughts about the things that they are asked to do and might be hesitant about accepting more challenges. The struggles that they feel at this juncture in life can keep them from wanting to move forward. A person's performance might start to decline as a result of perceived pressure to perform.

General Fears

Everyone has their own fears and worries about problems they may encounter in life, some minor, and some developing into major concerns. The greatest detriment to fear is that it often creates paralysis for doing anything.

The main problem of the Jonah Complex is that a person can become afraid of what success might bring. Success typically brings about more positives than negatives, but it is the negatives that people may start to think about above all else.

A person who has attained all the vital needs at the bottom of the Maslow pyramid might feel that he or she has everything they need for life. This keeps that person from being motivated or wanting to excel. Some of the fears include the worry that when one climbs higher in life, they will not be able to enjoy what they had in the past. That person may think that further success will take them away from their family or decrease the freedom to do various things they had enjoyed before. This is a sign of how attached people might be to one part of Maslow's pyramid. A person might be connected to a certain point and feels as though everything is fine. There might be a fear that going further up the pyramid will make it harder for a person to live life or to maintain the rest of the pyramid. This, in turn, keeps that person from feeling motivated and wanting to keep on moving toward something new.

Some people are afraid that they will make huge mistakes if they try for more success. With more duties and work to do, it might be easy for someone to feel overwhelmed. The added pressure might make it harder for that person to feel happy.

People might fear success because they regret not getting there sooner. Although anyone could take any path toward success in life, some people might believe that they would have wasted their lives because they did not do more to achieve more success.

The positives of success include recognition from other people, added earnings, and a better sense of security. It is very easy for people who struggle with the Jonah Complex to ignore those points. A person will begin to feel that there is no real reason to keep on working or accept more challenges. People who do not think about those benefits will struggle with the Jonah Complex as they feel uncertain about how they will be able to handle the success that could come about if they work harder.

How to Get Beyond the Jonah Complex

There are ways to overcome the Jonah Complex and to stop fearing success. The main point for getting past the complex is to help people see that they can succeed and that there is nothing to worry about. If anything, the Jonah Complex might be based on unrealistic attitudes and ideas.

Being Realistic

The first step toward self-actualization and success is to look at the worries one has. The problem with the Jonah Complex is that many of the things that people think about are not connected to reality. It can become extremely hard for people to think realistically and positively. It is a situation that has to be explored to see what can be done to resolve one's issues and emotional problems.

Realism is vital to help people understand that some of the things they are thinking might actually be incorrect. A good way to correct one's worries is to take a careful look at some of these issues and to see what can be done to resolve the problems that a person might have developed over time.

A few points should be explored at this juncture:

- How will one's family and friends respond to what is happening?

In most cases, those people will actually feel happy about someone attaining self-actualization and might be motivated to do the same.

- How is someone's life going to change?

There is a chance that a person's life will improve if they understand what can be done to be happy and positive. A realistic look at this might reveal that someone's success will lead to more opportunities for further success, better relationships with other people, and even the potential of earning more money.

- What are the worst things that could actually happen?

A person who is asked this question might mention unrealistic or irrational things. At this point, they should be reminded to start thinking about more positive and controllable things that can be done to improve one's life.

- What does a person think might keep them from deserving a goal?

This question often focuses on some of the worries that people hold in their minds. They might start to ask questions that are unrealistic or nonsensical without thinking about the positive aspects of what can happen with success and hard work.

- What is the true motivation for actually succeeding?

It helps to ask a person about what might happen in life and how things can change for the better. The goal is to let someone know that there is always going to be something worth considering.

- Is there something a person is doing to keep from actually succeeding, and what can be done to stop those issues from becoming worse?

Knowing how to resolve certain problems can make a difference when trying to figure out what changes to make and how things might be different in the future.

Look at Past Experiences

Sometimes things that have happened in the past make a real difference. Past experiences should be explored to remind a person why they were working toward self-realization in the first place. Sometimes this might give a person motivation once again.

There are more questions that need to be asked at this juncture. These questions concentrate mainly on the good things that are happening in one's life and what can be done to make certain experiences a little stronger and more worthwhile.

- What types of successes has one had in the past?

Asking about these successes at the start helps people to recognize what they can do to change their lives and move forward. The successes that are revealed at this point can guide a person to answer the next questions.

- How did other people react to the successes one had?

The odds are those people reacted in a positive way to those successes. They were probably happy with what someone had done.

- What things changed following certain successes?

The changes might be good things. These include things that made life a little easier. It could be feeling positive and in control of work. Maybe that person might have earned more money among other great things.

- What decisions might have caused certain positive things to happen?

There is always a chance that good things happened in the past to cause someone to feel a little better and happier about where one is going. The decisions that need to be made might be vital to understanding the things that are changing when positive things happen.

By working with these questions, a person will stop feeling fearful or worried about what might happen in the future. They will want to continue working toward a positive result.

Develop a Success Plan

There is always the potential for someone to come across new ideas or plans for work. A success plan can be developed after the positives associated with going forward are analyzed and considered in detail. Having a success plan helps a person to stay motivated while knowing what performance metrics are important for one's work. This also creates a sensible roadmap to know what to do when trying to move forward and get something done the right way.

A plan should be prepared based on the fears that one has. The goal is to address those fears and to find ways to keep those problems from being more of an issue than they have to be. There are many things that people can do to stay motivated:

1. Make a schedule.

One of the most common issues people have that often contributes to the Jonah Complex involves one's schedule. A person might not be aware of how to manage their schedule and become fearful of not having enough time to do the things that need to be done. By using a sensible schedule, it becomes easier to create a sense of timing for certain tasks. The schedule might include when to start working and when to stop each day. It might also set aside certain days of the week or hours per day to spend time with family or friends.

2. Understand priorities.

Priorities include not only what is more important for their lives but also what things in their lives they deem as relevant and worth focusing on. By deciding what to concentrate on, it becomes easier for people to feel more confident about the tasks at hand.

3. Establish many backup plans for multiple situations.

Sometimes people struggle with keeping their lives in check because they have not created backup plans. Nothing in life goes exactly as planned. Situations will pop up that were not expected and having backup plans help reorganize priorities and make it possible to handle surprises. When you are scheduling your time, you must also think about out-of-the-ordinary situations that might interfere and throw your schedule off. Many backup plans can include delaying certain tasks, which will necessitate. The key is to be flexible and be willing to rearranging your schedule and priorities.

By using a good plan for success, you will have a newfound sense of organization and control over the tasks that need to be done.

Recognize Who Really Has the Problem

An interesting part of success is that sometimes the problems that one has are unfounded or the problems are those of someone else.

It is true that there are cases where people will react negatively to someone's success. However, a person can become motivated by not thinking about him or herself as the problem. Rather, that person can recognize that the other people in society who are upset are the ones who have problems. Those people might have felt very successful in the past and are unhappy that other people may become more successful than them. The key is to avoid people who might try to hold others back because of how successful they are.

Knowing how to handle the fear of success is critical. It takes a great deal of motivation to avoid the problems that come with not wanting to succeed. There are better ways for someone to handle the worries that come with the Jonah Complex.

How Long Does It Take?

There are no real standards as to how long it takes for a person to get over the Jonah Complex. Some people can easily get beyond the complex in just a few weeks. In other cases, it takes regular conditioning and analysis over a few months to get someone past that issue. Working against the Jonah Complex might become a continuous process just as well. Although one person might have developed beyond the complex after a few weeks or months of effort, it is necessary to look at what can be done to keep the complex from returning and it takes a lot of effort.

Chapter 8 – The ERG Theory

Although Maslow's theory has long been seen as one of the more valuable theories for people to follow, it is not necessarily the only concept. Motivation and performance can work in many forms without set rules as to how well they are to be laid out. That is where the next major theory comes into play.

Motivation is influenced by the needs that people have. It is through those needs that people are motivated to do things. One theory that can be utilized to understand some of these needs is the ERG theory.

This is one of the more basic aspects of motivation as it focuses on the basic needs that people require to be met. The ERG theory was first established by Clayton Alderfer as a series of classes that concentrated on some of the things that people need in their lives.

The theory expands upon Maslow's hierarchy of needs. Alderfer arranged the hierarchy into three simple sections that analyze the main reasons why people exist and what they require. This is used to understand what causes people to be motivated.

To some, the ERG theory might actually be a simplification of everything that Maslow has discussed. However, it is actually different in a way. The ERG theory states that a person could go from one end of the pyramid to the other at any time. That person might start at the top and then go to the bottom, for instance. The streamlined nature of the pyramid makes it easy for a person to change attitudes and redirect their paths.

The Three Parts

The ERG is an acronym for Existence, Relatedness, and Growth.

1. Existence

The existence needs are those needs a person has for living. A person is often more likely to be motivated by these needs above all else.

The safety and physiological needs that Maslow introduced in his theory are part of the ERG theory.

The existence needs include things like being able to have a good home and to be healthy. A person's stability is a necessity to ensure that a person's existence is not threatened. The existence part of the theory is on the bottom of the pyramid. The things that one would require at this juncture are the most important.

2. Relatedness

Relatedness refers to how well a person is capable of maintaining and managing relationships with other people. This includes not only being recognized by those people but also for finding romance or at least a professional connection with someone that can last for years.

This part of the theory focuses on the Maslow's esteem factors. When a person is able to handle one's existence needs, they can get in touch with others and address their relatedness needs.

The relationships that people can develop may help them with growing and doing more with their lives. They might discover that there are many people in a community who can help them. By working with only the best relationships, it becomes easier for a person to start working and to feel motivated as there are some people in their life who care. It is the feeling of being with someone that can make a real difference when it comes to being motivated.

3. Growth

Growth is the ability to expand one's horizons and values. The concept of self-actualization can be found in this part of the ERG theory.

After a person has attained their basic needs for survival and has established relationships, it is time for that person to grow and there is a greater chance to thrive and succeed in life.

The type of growth for each individual is varied. A person might become more creative and have wonderful ideas to enhance their lives and the lives of others. Maybe a person is willing to take on new responsibilities at work. The possibilities are endless. This is the stage of one's life where they can actualize their dreams, influence others, and make substantial contributions to society.

These three parts of the ERG theory are important, but it is even more important to consider how a person might move from one part of the pyramid to another. As the next part of this chapter will explain, the ERG theory allows for a more flexibility about where a person might go and how they are capable of developing and evolving in life.

What Makes the ERG Theory Different?

Naturally, the ERG theory is similar to Maslow's hierarchy. It focuses on growth and development while concentrating on the basic needs that a person has at the beginning. The ERG theory has fewer tiers in its pyramid than what Maslow introduced, but it is a distinct theory in its own right:

1. When a high-level need is satisfied, it will become more important for a person to fulfill the low-level needs.

There might be cases where a person's needs for relatedness or growth could be met before anything relating to existence is met. Whenever this happens, it becomes all the more important for a person to find a way to satisfy the need for the basics in life. This could happen when there is a need to stay healthy, to handle a new job, or maybe the ability to purchase better shelter with the money earned by an extended period of work.

When the low-level needs are not managed well, it becomes harder for the high-level needs to stay supported. A person who cannot get the shelter or food one needs will not feel ready to be creative or to maintain the emotional relationships that one wants to pursue. It is a frustrating part of life, but it cannot be ignored.

2. A person can go from one level of the ERG pyramid to another. This is different from Maslow's pyramid that describes movement from one level to another as difficult.

When a person feels a need to grow, they might want to try and manage one's relatedness needs, for instance. A worker might have a desire to grow and apply for a higher position, but also need to satisfy their relatedness needs by having better relationships with other people in the workplace to have allies who are willing to provide support.

Let's say that an athlete has the proper basic needs that he requires to stay healthy and ready to compete. He has a home to live in, the nutritional support he needs to work to his best potential and a healthy body. While he has the option to get into the relatedness part of the pyramid and find people who can support him, he still has the option to choose growth. He might focus on preparing for special events or working to compete in events to win or at least improve upon his overall performance.

The athlete still has the opportunity to move into the relatedness part of the ERG theory. He can find a sponsor who can financially fund his athletic efforts or maybe a romantic partner who is there to support and inspire him. The athlete can still go into the second or third parts of the pyramid at any time. The only real requirement is that he completes the first part of the pyramid so he has the basics needed for competing. Of course, he would still have to sustain the necessities and keep that first part intact in order to continue to compete.

3. The ERG theory lets a person work on the highest parts of the pyramid first.

The concept of the starving artist can be clearly identified through the ERG theory. An artist might work to create musical albums or fine pieces of art. He might concentrate on expanding his horizons and growing as an artist before he is able to earn the money he requires or before he finds the relationships that he needs for success or for personal comfort.

Every person will have their own path on the ERG pyramid, which is much different from the Maslow pyramid. It is just as important for motivation as it shows that anyone can be motivated by various factors.

How This Can Be Used In the Workplace

The ERG theory can be applied by a manager in the workplace by recognizing that employees might have several needs at any given time. While people might have the need for shelter and money, they also may have needs to grow and advance in their lives so they can be more productive.

The greatest concern for a manager is that all three parts of the pyramid might be hard to satisfy. For instance, a person might not be given the opportunity to advance or earn more money while on the job, thus leading that person to relate to other workers just to manage their personal needs. That person could focus on their personal needs instead of focusing on the job; this makes it harder for a business to function properly.

This example shows that the worker is ignoring the growth part of the ERG theory and is focusing on relatedness. Eventually, they might move into the existence needs by looking toward earning more money to manage the relationships they have established.. This can happen in spite of not having gone through the growth part of the pyramid.

The ERG theory shows that workplaces and other environments have to satisfy a wide range of needs that people have. Although an employee might have managed certain needs, they could possibly have newer and more important needs.

The best thing that a business can do is to recognize that every person in the workplace has their own attitudes and ideas about advancement. Some people might feel that they can advance further in their lives if they concentrate on developing their skills. Others will simply feel they can develop if the basics in their lives are met. The concept of motivation will be different, so it will be critical for businesses to consider how each person in the workplace feels about their work life and where their priorities lie.

How Can the Three Sections Link To Each Other?

Sometimes a person's satisfaction with individual parts of the ERG pyramid will allow them to move from one part to another, and regress as well. The three sections in the ERG pyramid can be analyzed based on how they connect with one another:

1. When a person is satisfied with one's existence needs, it is easier to progress forward to relatedness. The existence needs may also be strengthened or reinforced with more basic needs developing when support is added.

2. The relatedness needs allow for a person to not only progress toward growth needs but to also regress back to being concerned about existence needs. Reinforcement of the relatedness needs is possible, but it is not as frequently used as it is with the existence.

3. Growth needs do not have any progression as this is as high on the pyramid as one can go. A person can reinforce one's desires, but there is also a potential for a person to revert or regress back to one of the other two parts of the pyramid.

The ability to go forward or backward within the ERG theory is vital for people to consider. Using the pyramid, employers can understand how a person's attitudes might change based on where they are on that pyramid.

More importantly, people should notice that the ERG theory allows people to move from one aspect of motivation to another. A business or school can analyze what inspires people and review where others might be in their lives to get an idea of what is motivating them. This, in turn, makes it easier for particular decisions to be made based on what people might be influenced by and how they keep those influences under control and in check.

The ERG theory does more than just keep Maslow's hierarchy in a simplified layout with fewer details involved. The ERG theory also shows that there is an ability in all people to move to and from one part of the pyramid to another. The potential for people to have desires that cover all parts of the pyramid at once is also there as well. This part of the motivation is vital for helping to see what causes a person to act in certain ways and to stay active and involved in their field of work.

Chapter 9 – Theories X and Y

Management theory has been a critical part of running a business that many operators like to use. This is how a manager is capable of organizing and business and identifying the things that need to be done to make the business into a success. A vital part of a management theory is understanding how to get employees motivated to actually do their jobs. This is where Theories X and Y come into play.

This part of the psychology of motivation focuses on how a manager is going to handle a work environment. It is about how people are going to behave in a certain manner.

Theories X and Y concentrate on two types of people - people who might not want to work and those who are excited about working. These two types of people are motivated by different attitudes or actions. A business that knows how to corral its employees and manage them accordingly will have an easier time succeeding and moving forward.

Theories X and Y focus on not only how people behave but also what makes them stronger and capable of handling certain tasks. This is all based on the propensities that people have toward work and what they can accomplish.

The Basics

Douglas McGregor, a 20th Century psychologist, used Theories X and Y to understand how business management functions might be utilized. These points can be summarized in a simple way to understand how motivation works:

- X: this person refuses to do the work; that person has their arms crossed in an X pattern to indicate a refusal to work

- Y: this person wants to work; it is symbolized by a person holding their arms up to show a strong interest in accepting work.

Theory X is the belief that the people in a work environment might not have much desire to actually do the work one is given to do. Theory Y is the assumption that people will want to work and are actively ready to be involved.

The two theories have unique points for motivation that help businesses to see why individual workers might be inspired in many ways. However, the two theories are very different from one another. These are based on different assumptions that might be held with regards to individuals in the workplace.

Theory X

Theory X focuses on the belief that the workers in an environment are not excited about working and do not have much ambition. They might try to skirt their way around or avoid their duties. In most cases, the workers are more focused on their own internal goals and not on the goals of the business.

A manager who operates under Theory X will focus on actively controlling the employees. The manager might think that the employees are dull and will not notice that they are being controlled. It is up to the manager to find a way to convince the employees that their jobs are important and that their careers can move forward if they just consider what they can do to help a business grow.

Employees who are handled under Theory X are interpreted as just wanting security. That is, they might be motivated to work simply because they will have something to do and will actually earn enough income. What is even more interesting is that those people might not be all that motivated to work because they do not have many ambitions. For some, the jobs that they have are as good as it is going to get for them.

The control within Theory X focuses on motivating people by letting them know that there is one central group in charge of things. These employees might be motivated by the belief that they will have to be careful with what they are doing if they want to keep their jobs.

In addition, Theory X motivates people into doing the same tasks many times over. The goal is for the manager to keep the workplace organized with a standard setup for just one thing to be done. This will involve trying to get all the employees to do as they are told with no questions asked.

Theory X is a valuable part of the motivation that can work in larger environments where there are more people. These include people who might be focused on extremely specific or particular fields of work that are not that detailed or complicated. In fact, the process might work well for unskilled labor.

The main concern here is that the people who work in a Theory X environment are ones that are motivated not so much by work and accomplishment but more by money. Although this might sound like a cold way of operating a business, it is still a process that has to be considered because it can help management get the most out of the employees' work.

Theory X is not always something that people like to be involved with because it focuses on people who might not want to work. It is critical for management to use Theory X to know what they can do to at least get the people in the workplace to be productive and active.

Theory Y

Theory Y is a part of the motivation that is focused on people who might be interested in their work. This is often seen as an ideal situation for work because the people involved might really have a strong interest in working. They want to keep on working with the belief that by consistently working hard, it becomes easier to stay positive and ready to get to work.

A manager will operate Theory Y with the assumption that the people in the workplace are ready to work and are very interested in what the business has to offer. In some cases, the employees will focus more on getting a business to grow than their ability to make money. Of course, the business will help the workers to earn more money or at least have a strong sense of job security.

It is typically not as hard to motivate people who work under Theory Y than it is to handle those on Theory X. With Theory Y, the people are interested in working and seem to have more enthusiasm for work. Employers can benefit from this provided that the working environment is controlled and easy to work with.

Employees who can conform to the Theory Y motivation are often treasured more than those who fall into the Theory X category. Theory Y workers will recognize how important the work they do is to the company. They will also be more responsible and will hold themselves accountable in cases where they do not do as well in their work as one might have hoped.

The motivational aspect of Theory Y focuses on allowing employees to do more for their lives and to keep on working toward the goals that they want to attain. With Theory Y, the manager lets people know that they are fully responsible and that they have the right to control what happens, thus causing people to become motivated.

The extent to which a person will be motivated through Theory Y will vary according to each employee. One employee might be motivated by helping the company to grow and thrive by doing their portion of the work. Some employees might be motivated by what more they can earn if they do their best and continue producing to a high standard. Others might be motivated by the fact that their functions in the workplace might make an impact on whether or not a business succeeds; that is, a person who fails will harm the business and its reputation.

With Theory Y, people are asked to complete their tasks. Organizational issues can be resolved as people will bring their skills together to solve the problems they might face. The teamwork that is encouraged at this point will make a real difference.

The most important part of Theory Y is that the hands-off approach to management will motivate people to achieve certain objectives. People tend not to be lazy, work together well, and do not postpone or ignore their responsibilities. This process can make a tremendous difference in how well a business is run and what can be accomplished.

Theory Y motivation works well for smaller businesses where it is easier to corral the employees so that they can understand one another. The types of businesses that can benefit from Theory Y motivation include call centers and other small office settings and retail stores that with a sizable and diverse array of customers or clients.

It is much easier to get people to feel positive about their work and to have a more free-wheeling attitude when Theory Y is used. Theory X would work in cases where it is hard to gage each employee, the tasks are regimented and repetitive, employees can rely on one person in charge, and there is not much flexibility in how the job is done.

Chapter 10 – The Two-Factor Theory

The satisfaction that one has within one's job can be very important. When a person feels satisfied with their work, it becomes easier to want to keep on working and to move toward an overall goal. The two-factor theory is a part of the motivation that may influence how a person stays confident and engaged.

This psychological concept was introduced by Frederick Herzberg as an expansion of Maslow's theory. He argues that one's satisfaction and dissatisfaction in work are two points that are separate from one another.

Herzberg states that the presence of incentives will impact how satisfied a person is at work. Meanwhile, another person will become dissatisfied with that same line of work. The psychological point is that an employer would have to find ways to target individuals according to what motivates them. When an employer sees what triggers feelings of satisfaction or feelings of unhappiness at work, that employer could offer more support to the unhappy employee.

Motivators

The two factors that are to be used in the two-factor theory are motivators and hygiene factors.

Motivators are defined by Herzberg as the concepts that actually motivate a person. These are concepts that are rooted in one's job. These motivators often include things like:

- Any achievements one can complete

- The possible recognition of a job well done

- The potential for a person to grow and enter a better and higher-paying position

- How that person can advance in one's career

- The responsibilities that come with a job

- How well the job can be completed

Employers can use these motivators to get ideas of how people behave. They can notice that all employees have their own inspirations that make them want to do well in their jobs and in their lives.

For instance, an architect might be inspired to complete a task to design a new residential community. She might be inspired to design it to show that she is talented and will rise above her peers. She might also feel that by producing the best possible environment for living, she could be given work for more advanced and complicated tasks.

She might not be the only one competing for a better position. She might have a contender who is interested in the recognition he might get from completing his task but also has a desire to advance his career. It is clear that people will have their own individual inspirations that will cause them to go forward and put a lot of effort into completing their tasks.

Hygiene Factors

Hygiene factors are not necessarily going to cause a person to feel motivated, but they will discourage motivation if they are absent. These factors must be present for people to feel that there is a purpose to a job. Some of the hygiene factors include:

- Policies or rules that people must follow in the workplace

- Any managerial or supervising efforts involved

- Salaries to pay out

- Job security

- How well a job allows people to balance their work and personal lives

- How good the working conditions are

Hygiene factors have to be present to keep people from feeling a lack of motivation. When people notice that there are enough of these factors, they will know that they are at least getting something out of the work they are putting in.

Let's go back to the example of the two competing architects. Although they have their own individual motivational factors for why they want to perform well, they might have a few concerns that would keep them from completing the task if those needs are not actually met. For instance, both of them might be worried about their job security or how well they are being paid. The two of them would feel inhibited if they notice that they are not being paid sufficiently. Problems with not being able to get in touch with their families might be a serious problem for some people. The concerns that these people have could prove to be dramatic and can keep them from going forward and doing their best.

The greatest problem is that it is often easy for managers and other business operators to assume that hygiene factors are going to directly motivate people. Herzberg argues that the motivators are separate from the hygiene factors that, when missing, de-motivate people. Therefore, a workplace must not only provide the hygiene factors that they require but also attend to the concerns that they might have that could cause them to lose motivation.

How Can Motivational Factors Be Increased?

Herzberg proposes three points in his theory that encourage motivational factors to increase:

1. People can have more complicated job roles.

In this case, people might be allowed to work with more responsibilities and duties in their positions regardless of where they are on the company ladder. Those who are given many things to do will feel as though they can go anywhere in their positions and that there is always going to be something worthwhile for them to do.

Offering more things to do can also give people a sense of job security. If a person has more things to do, it reinforces the idea that there is always going to be a need for them to continue working. This allows a person to feel that they have job security and not at risk of losing their pay.

2. Individual jobs can be rotated.

Job roles might be shifted or rotated so that an employee doesn't get bored by doing the same task over and over. An example might be a worker at a retail store. A worker might be told to work on tasks like handling people on the sales floor or managing the inventory. During busy times, that person could also be asked to work in another department where customers are picking up products that they ordered online. The variety of jobs that the employee is asked to do will make it easier for them to feel confident in one's job because of the responsibilities that come with it. The perceived belief that the employee is more valuable to the business because of their ability to change tasks and still perform is bound to make an impact on the employer. This gives the employee added confidence in their abilities and their flexibility.

3. Continuing education is a must.

It might be easy for people to feel a lack of motivation if they feel that what they are working at a job that is going to be the same forever. Each task must feel new or unique in some way for a person to feel motivated. This includes allowing people to handle many lines of work at any given time.

The retail employee mentioned before could be taught how to use new technical devices on the sales floor, how to handle some new line of merchandize or other service being offered. The key is to get that person to learn more about the many tasks that need to be done in the workplace. By giving someone that knowledge, that person to want to do more and be proficient.

Should Not Be Treated As a Universal Theory

Although the concepts introduced in the two-factor theory might be worthwhile, that does not mean they will work for every single person. There should never be an assumption that the happiest and most motivated people are going to produce more than anyone else. Those who might feel dissatisfied might perform well but could do even better when some of the hygiene factors that they are missing are actually fulfilled and satisfied.

Meanwhile, every person will be motivated differently. Understanding what might motivate someone and how well that person might work in a certain situation is vital to the overall success in the workplace. It can be a challenge at times, but it is a critical concept for any business to follow.

Other Limits

There are a few limits associated with the two-factor theory:

- No two situations are the same. There is a chance one variable might be more important than the other for a time.

- Every person has certain values that are different from what others might hold.

- The theory focuses more on white-collar tasks.

Although this theory identifies how professional employees work, it does not focus on blue-collar workers. These include people who might not be motivated much and are just focused on working specific tasks for a certain amount of money without any thoughts of advancement.

- The theory focuses more on how employees react. It might not be influenced by the reasons for why individual employees are pleased or upset.

Understanding the two-factor theory helps businesses identify what they can do to succeed and how they are capable of operating and improving. Those who follow the theory can understand what it takes to help a business grow and how to keep the employees positive and happy while feeling encouraged as well.

Chapter 11 – The 16 Basic Desires

Some of the points that directly motivate people are the things that make them happy. Everyone has their own ideas of what makes them happy and to feel positive in their lives. These points for happiness can be summarized through what is known as the 16 Basic Desires. This is a theory of motivation that was developed by psychology professor Steven Reiss in the 1990s.

The theory was established during a time period when Reiss was hospitalized. He noticed that even though the nurses who were taking care of him had lots of work to do and were often placed into stressful situations, they felt very motivated and happy with their lives. Those nurses especially loved the work they were doing.

This led Reiss to ask about what causes a person to feel happy. He studied thousands of people to find out what triggers them into feeling happy. Overall, he found a total of sixteen values and needs that people have that cause them to stay motivated. These are what he calls the 16 Basic Desires of motivation.

To determine what desires a person has, it might help to have that person take an appropriate test. This would entail looking into the various feelings and attitudes that someone might have toward particular actions. The test that may be used will be discussed a little later in this chapter.

What makes this theory important is that there are no rules as to how many of these desires a person might express. A person could have just one of these desires at a time. In other cases, that person might have all sixteen of them. It only takes just one for a person to feel motivated and encouraged to perform to one's potential. Knowing how these desires are organized can be vital to understanding how people will behave in certain ways.

The Desires

These 16 Basic Desires can be divided up into a series of categories. These focus on everything from the general everyday needs that people have to the social considerations that one might want to live under. Each point also has its own basic value with a positive aspect attached.

The desires are divided based on the general needs that people have, their personal needs, and their social desires. Each person places a greater weight on certain concepts, but they all focus on what they can do to make their lives more meaningful and worthwhile.

An interesting part of these desires is that they could relate to Maslow's needs based on how they are organized by importance. In the ERG theory, people could experience any of these desires at any time while certain sections might be ignored. The survival necessities are still what people will have a need to fulfill, but everything listed here could be used in some fashion.

Basics

The basics focus on the things that a person needs above all else. These are the first desires that people try to meet before they can go anywhere. People typically spend more time thinking about these desires without thinking about the problems they might run into and the fears that may result from what one might do.

1. Eating

A person will have a need to eat regularly. This might also include a need to eat healthily and to keep one's body from suffering from any serious physical threats. Sometimes this focuses on just trying to stay satisfied and to keep from being distracted by hunger.

General Goal: To take in sustenance.

Long-Term Goal: To feel satiated.

2. Family

Someone might have a desire to have children. This includes the desire to have a healthy body to actually support the ability to have children.

General Goal: To have a family with a partner and children; having children might be optional for some, so there is a general goal to at least feel happy being in a relationship.

Long-Term Goal: To feel the love from others or to at least be appreciated; this may be accomplished with or without children.

3. Physical Exercise

Physical exercise can involve strengthening one's body and muscles or improving heart functions.

General Goal: To stay fit.

Long-Term Goal: To feel energetic and active in one's life; this includes avoiding atrophy.

<u>Personal Needs</u>

Personal needs are things that relate not so much to the body but rather for the mind.

4. Romance

People might have a need to fall in love. This can be long and short-term relationships, but the key is to be happy with the relationship or relationships one has chosen.

General Goal: To experience sensuality, possibly through sex.

Long-Term Goal: To feel happy and joyful about the act of sex or feel positive about one's romantic partner.

5. Curiosity

There is always a desire among many people to learn new things. They might want to see how certain ideas work or if they can change their lives by engaging in new actions.

General Goal: To develop new ideas.

Long-Term Goal: To be amazed by everything that one tries or to expand one's horizons.

6. Honor

Many people around the world are motivated to respect certain codes of honor or behavior. They feel a need to follow each rule that they have adopted no matter how detailed it might be or how difficult it is for someone to follow it.

General Goal: To express a sense of duty.

Long-Term Goal: To be loyal to another; this might be expressing loyalty to a family member, a romantic partner, or an employer.

7. Independence

A person might want to be free to make choices. That person wants to set their own course in life. This includes knowing their role without being judged.

General Goal: To be self-reliant.

Long-Term Goal: To be free from judgments or hassles.

8. Order

Some people may a desire for order in their lives. This includes knowing that everything has a place. The order that someone establishes can ensure there are no problems and that life is not chaotic. This includes making sure things are predictable in some way.

General Goal: To be stable.

Long-Term Goal: To feel comfortable and to know what to expect from life.

9. Power

A person might want to influence others. This includes having control over other people or simply being able to impose their will on others. Sometimes the desire for power might lead to a person simply wanting to be recognized as being powerful.

General Goal: To become a leader and to achieve things.

Long-Term Goal: To become self-efficient; this includes being recognized by others as being someone powerful and in control.

10. Saving

Some people prefer to save or collect. The belief is that those who have more things are happier. Whatever a person decides to save or collect needs to be considered to see if they are absolutely necessary.

General Goal: To be frugal and in control of one's life.

Long-Term Goal: To own more things and to have control over one's assets; this includes having an understanding of the reasons why those things are needed.

11. Tranquility

Tranquility is a feeling of safety and peace. A person will want to avoid fearful things or anything that causes anxiety. There exists a desire to stay comfortable and less likely to be harmed.

General Goal: To stay cautious and under control.

Long-Term Goal: To feel relaxed and not be triggered by any a change in situations.

12. Vengeance

Motivation often comes from people wanting to succeed. They might feel a need to retaliate against others who have slighted them in the past. A person might try to win and be dominant over someone else. In most cases, this focuses on proving people wrong. In other cases, it is more about wanting to show others that they were right and others were wrong.

General Goal: To simply win.

Long-Term Goal: To feel vindicated in one's words, thoughts, or actions.

Social Points

The social points are desires that people have that relate to their relationships with others. They want to be seen by others as being strong. The inner thoughts of one's relationships with other people are not as important as the personal interactions that become all the more essential and vital.

13. Acceptance

People often try to be accepted by others. They want to be appreciated without being judged by others for who they are or what skills they have, or the lack of such skills.

General Goal: To feel encouraged.

Long-Term Goal: To establish a sense of self-confidence that others cannot take away.

14. Idealism

A person might want to improve society by creating a sense of justice and support for others. These include those who might have been harmed by society in the past.

General Goal: To be fair.

Long-Term Goal: To be compassionate.

15. Social Contact

People often look for friends to appreciate and be in contact with.

General Goal: To feel as though one belongs somewhere.

Long-Term Goal: To have fun with other people.

16. Status

Status is the need for attention or a need to be more important when compared with others. Everyone has their own attitudes for what they feel relates to positivity and status.

General Goal: To develop a better reputation.

Long-Term Goal: To be regarded as important.

These sixteen desires are important to understanding in any person at school or in the workplace. When a person's desires are understood, it becomes easier to discover what causes a person to be inspired and to feel a desire to perform work.

How can these desires be utilized or at least determined for each person? The Reiss profile test can be utilized to help understand what might cause people to feel certain desires and to see how intense people might feel about some of them. After all, some people might experience certain desires more than others.

The Reiss Profile

No two people are alike in terms of their basic desires. Some people are overly concerned about the essentials for their lives; others might focus a little more on some of the more urgent or demanding needs.

The 16 Basic Desires can be measured in an individual person through what is known as a Reiss profile. This is a profile that ranks these sixteen points based on their intensity.

The Reiss profile shows each of these points and measures them in one of three ways. A person might have a lesser need for one of these desires. That person might also have a high demand for certain desires and will want to work harder to attain them. There are also times when a person has an average rating and could live either with or without one of those desires.

The profile is often administered by an extensive questionnaire. This would have to be administered over a long period of time and could entail multiple tests at different times.

The measurements can help determine what attitudes someone might have about different concepts. For instance, a person who scores well on the power attribute will have a real desire to be a leader. Someone who is high on the Vengeance profile might feel very competitive or want to prove a point. That person might not be compatible as a leader due to a clash of attitudes.

The test could last for a long time, but it is best to use a few dozen questions at a time. Software programs may be used to generate results based on the certain parameters that are reviewed and used in the test. Working with a good program will generate results that can be reliable.

Basic Applications of the Profile

The Reiss profile measurements will identify some of the attributes that might motivate people. These include how people might value power and control over some of the personal things that they need in their lives.

This could also help understand how compatible people might be with one another. The results of one's Reiss profile test could be compared with others in the same workplace to see how well a person could work in certain situations and if that person is appropriate for hire or where they would best fit in the workplace. This creates a better overall team and also reduces the risk of a conflict.

This may also identify conflicts within the workplace. Sometimes these conflicts might become disruptive due to issues surrounding people who have different personalities or desires. By using the profile measurement, a business can identify the problems in a workplace and decide on solutions to resolve the issue before it can become more problematic than it might already be.

The 16 Basic Desires theory outlines valuable concepts that can help people identify how the psychology of motivation works and why people might behave as they do in various situations.

Chapter 12 – Resistance

It is very easy for people to feel unmotivated. They could feel a lack of encouragement and no real desire to try and do something of value. This could make it more difficult to feel confident and positive about their lives.

Resistance often occurs in many people because they want to change things in their lives. In most cases, this happens because they are dissatisfied with the jobs they are asked to perform. Most people might notice resistance in the form of protests when people are opposed to certain things that they are not interested in doing. There are many ways how resistance might be demonstrated.

It is also easy to motivate people when the main points of resistance in the human mind are identified and then countered. This is to take advantage of knowing how the brain functions and will respond to various forms of stimuli.

A General Review of Resistance

Resistance is defined by Sigmund Freud as when a person is trying to consciously keep from moving toward something. This could be due to any kind of attitude one has. In some cases, a person might be blocking memories. In other cases, that person is simply fearful and uncertain about what might happen.

Someone is on the verge of being motivated and ready to do something when that person starts to resist. This might be a sign that a person is ready to make a real change and initiate an action.

Resistance is an indicator that a person is close to actually feeling motivated. When a person gets close to changing one's mind, it becomes easier for that person to do something. The goal is to ensure that a person is willing to move forward and is not going to be judgmental over something that could happen later. By countering a person's resistance, it becomes easier for a person to want to move forward when they are motivated to do something they did not want to do in the first place.

Three Vital Aspects of Resistance

All people show resistance differently. It is important to notice how resistance is exhibited to understand what causes the human mind to act as it does and how to change attitudes or values.

Autonomy

The first concept relating to resistance involves autonomy. This refers to when a person might resist wanting to do something by being told they have to do it. For instance, a homeowner might find a need to renovate his master bathroom because some fixtures in that room are wearing out. He might say, "I have to fix this space." This is a sign that he is not really willing to fix the bathroom. He feels as though he is being forced to take care of the issue due to the condition of that room. He does not want to work because he does not see much enjoyment in it.

This problem can be resolved by helping a person to change how they think. The key is to concentrate on the benefits that come with the task at hand. This will change one's mindset from "I have to" to "I will", thus making a person be motivated.

In this example, the homeowner might begin to realize that fixing up his bathroom will offer several benefits. He may notice that the risk of further damages will be reduced after he fixes the problem in that room. He may also realize that his bathroom will look nicer and might even be a little more functional after the renovation is finished. Even more so, he may realize that the value of his property could increase.

By recognizing the benefits, it becomes easier for someone to break through that barrier of resistance. That person will start to feel motivated and actually finish a certain task and be pleased about it.

Value

There is always going to be some kind of benefit of completing a task or action even if that person resists it at the start. Even if that person notices how important something might be and how great it is to get to the next level, there is another point of resistance that might get in the way. This relates to one's belief that something is not going to be as valuable as what one might have seen in the past.

The value of something can make a difference when looking at what someone is thinking about a certain action. For instance, a person might not feel right about a task that is different from what they might want to do.

Let's say that a secretary in the workplace is being asked to work overtime. She might not feel motivated and will resist because she does not feel that the overtime is right for her. She might think that she needs to spend time with her family or to do other things that she had hoped to do instead.

However, the problems that she has can be resolved by allowing her to reorganize her tasks and adjust her efforts. For instance, she might overcome that resistance by changing some of her values around. She might move some of the extra hours she wanted to spend with her family to the next week or other time when she is able to have time off, thus giving her the opportunity to be with her family.

She might be encouraged if she thinks about the future benefits. For instance, she might notice that by working overtime, she can get the money she needs to take the family on a vacation at some point in the future. She might also receive a better performance review, which could lead to an increase in her pay and possibly a promotion to a personal assistant or managerial position that she might have been wanting.

Those who feel that certain actions or ideas are not going to be worth enough will not feel motivated because they do not see value in whatever they are being encouraged to do. Those who see the value of the benefits can overcome resistance.

The general value of an action is essential. Those who feel that there is a strong value attached to a job will feel more confident and willing to do it and more willing to listen to suggestions.

Ability

The third aspect of resistance is one's abilities. A person might not want to do a task because that person feels a general sense of inability to actually complete a task. That person might be distracted by the potential of failure as a result of being unable to do something.

Those who do feel they are capable of completing certain tasks are more likely to feel motivated. They know that they are equipped to handle a task and that they are not afraid of what might occur when they are working on something. By understanding one's overall ability, it becomes easier for a person to start working and   complete a task.

Let's go back to that example from earlier about the homeowner trying to renovate his master bathroom. He might resist the task because he feels that he is not capable or does not have the skills needed to do the renovations. He might feel that he might cause more damage to his bathroom and cost even more to renovate the room.

The distraction of failing would be a significant problem. He would be so preoccupied with failure that he would see no real value in doing the renovation. It is the perceived lack of one's ability that could keep the process from being completed.

A person can get beyond resistance by looking at how the effort will make an impact. When enough effort is put into the task at hand, the person completing it will get better with the process.

In addition, there is no need to worry about asking for assistance or looking for information on how to finish a task. That person can actually put in an effort to learn more about what can be done. This improves one's attitude toward a task and allows that person to keep moving forward while staying active and involved.

The homeowner looking to renovate his bathroom will learn more about how to complete the task at hand. By putting in the effort, he will improve his skills and the ability to finish the task. More importantly, he might notice that he always had the ability but was not convinced that he could do it. This makes him feel he could have done everything sooner if he had been afraid to try.

Resistance is always going to be a concern when it comes to motivation. People are always going to have their own problems and might not be comfortable with what they are asked to do. By identifying the main causes of resistance and knowing how to get past them, it becomes easier to get others to learn more about themselves and to get beyond the mental blocks and issues they might have.

Overcoming Resistance

The three aspects of resistance are often hard to overcome. When a workplace or other group finds ways to control resistance, it becomes easier for that place to be productive and successful. A few tips can be used for helping to keep resistance from being a dramatic threat that could hurt one's ability to work properly:

1. Be descriptive of the things that might happen in the workplace or any other environment.

The things that could happen should include a combination of the end result of a task and the benefits that will come out of that result. The discussion is important because people who know what is going to happen and why these things might happen will have an easier time with moving forward and being strong.

2. Discuss the benefits.

It is a necessity to look at how the individual is going to benefit. Each person should be addressed as to what one can do to succeed and how a particular action will make it easier for them to move forward. A business should be as specific and direct about the benefits of something as possible.

3. Explain what can be done to overcome the resistance involved.

Giving detailed instructions on what one can do to get beyond the obstacles in one's way is necessary so that people become more likely to feel motivated if they understand what they are required to do.

4. Be willing to guide people through the entire process.

Getting past resistance is more than just giving people instructions. It also involves letting people know the steps needed to complete the task from start to finish. Knowing how people will act at certain times and how they might keep working hard toward something is important as it helps to watch for cases where people might start to resist once again.

5. Offer training if needed.

In addition to guidance, training might be required. Training can be provided to provide the skills that people need to complete the tasks at hand. This gives the person receiving the training confidence and less inclined to offer resistance.

By knowing what can be done to overcome resistance, it will become easier for someone to continue to move forward and be actively involved.

Chapter 13 – Understanding Willpower and the Link to Motivation

Anyone can become motivated. Knowing what inspires a person to act in a certain way is always important. It is even more important to look at how a person will maintain that motivation. This leads to another part of psychology, that being willpower.

Willpower is a part of the motivation that many people often forget about, but it is something that influences how effective the motivation can be. Willpower is the sense of control that a person has to either do something or to resist. Willpower relates to motivation in that it involves completing certain tasks. When a person is motivated, that person will want to take action, but willpower is also needed to complete that action.

Think about willpower as what someone might experience when trying to wake up. Sometimes a person does not have the willpower to actually get out of bed at a reasonable time and get to work. After a while, that person will find the willpower to get up and get to work. This could come from anything relating to an obligation to do things or simply a desire to complete a task because of the perceived benefits of doing so being strong. A lack of willpower might make the situation worse due to not being able to do what one wants to complete.

The greatest concern about willpower is that it is not something that lasts forever. A person will have limits for the willpower one might have. Someone might be motivated to do things and will use one's willpower to charge forward. That person will have gone through so many decisions and actions that it becomes harder for that person to feel motivated. Willpower starts to decline and eventually that person doesn't feel able to complete the task.

This is known as decision fatigue. All the choices being made and the emotional and mental stress that comes with those moves will keep someone from being ready to keep moving forward. Several strategies can still be used to keep the brain focused and motivated even when one's willpower runs out. The most important goal is to keep decision fatigue from being a significant problem.

Producing a Healthy Routine

A good part of motivation involves developing a routine. Even a person who is motivated to do something and to start working might not have enough willpower due to all those choices that have to be made. For instance, a person might be ready to wake up and get ready for work and, at the same time, there may be too many choices that the person might have to make. What shirt should he wear? What should he have for breakfast? What tasks should be tackled first? Who should he contact?

After a while, all those questions make it more difficult for someone to have a desire to work. A person will not have enough energy to keep one's motivation moving forward. This is where establishing a sensible routine comes in handy. Routines are valuable for motivation because they keep a person from having to make too many decisions or ask lots of questions during the day. This gives the person a better sense of willpower for actually finishing tasks.

The worker listed earlier might feel a little more motivated when he knows what to do and when to do it. For instance, he might know what he will have for breakfast and might have ideas for what he will wear. He may also have priorities over what he will do in the workplace each day without thinking too much about what he will and will not do. Because he does not have too many questions, he will feel a little more positive and will have the will to actually move forward. All the motivation that he had at the start of the day will persist and he will keep on working as well as he wants to.

The routine does not always have to be followed to the letter every day. Some variations may be allowed here and there if only to keep a person from doing the same things all the time. Having some changes in one's routine is always worth considering because it adds a bit of interest and intrigue to the day. The key is to avoid deviating too much from the routine. The goal is to keep a person from feeling confused or uncomfortable with a situation that might happen.

Review What's Important At the Start

Motivation starts to fade late in the day when one starts to feel fatigue. All that work and effort placed on certain things throughout the day will make it harder for a person to want to keep on working.

A key part of maintaining one's sense of willpower is to take a look at what is important above all others at the beginning of the routine. This includes looking into how certain actions might be done and how to maintain a good routine throughout the whole day.

Prioritizing the daily tasks sets the tasks in order. Deciding the importance of each task one has to do in the day is essential.

Get Rid of Unnecessary Stuff

Sometimes people struggle to keep their willpower intact because they are saddled with too many things in their lives.

They might struggle to keep their minds on the tasks at hand because they are too busy thinking about some of the extra things they want to do or what they feel they have to do.

The greatest concern is that sometimes the things that people want to do are completely unnecessary. They might add pressure so that the person is no longer willing to keep working. For instance, a person might be thinking about one's daily routine at the workplace. One of those steps might be stopping at a coffee shop to get something en route to work. Is that step necessary? Sometimes a problem like this might cause someone to waste too much time, thus impacting that person's willpower. The best thing to do is to encourage that person to say no to some things. By sticking with a better routine, it becomes easier for the brain to stay active and ready to do anything one wants to complete.

Willpower is critical for anyone who wants to move forward and to have the willpower needed to sustain one's motivation.

Chapter 14 – Cognitive Motivation

Cognitive thinking refers to how people are able to acquire knowledge and how they can use that information to their advantage. By taking in new knowledge, it becomes easier for a person to make decisions. This might be the use of logic and reasoning to decide the best things to do at any given time. Having a clear idea of what can work in a situation is a necessity to complete any task.

Cognitive motivation is how people use their minds to determine what is important to them. It is an extensive part of the motivation.

Understanding Cognitive Psychology

To have an understanding of how cognitive motivation works, it helps to see what makes cognitive psychology so distinct. This is a study of mental processes and how the human mind associates certain concepts change a person's attitudes or actions.

The key is to discover how people might respond to certain situations or make decisions that they feel are worthwhile and important to follow.

General Concepts

When using cognitive psychology to help people become motivated and to perform to their best standards, it is a necessity to look at a few general standards for working. Many basics can be seen in this field:

1. Goals may be established.

When goals are created, it becomes easier for people to move forward. They will understand that there are very specific things that they can do to succeed. They might become focused on those goals while knowing that they can succeed and go further in their work if they just think about some things that might change over time.

2. Connections are to be established.

The connections that people can use in cognitive psychology can entail any kind of reward or another benefit. Some incentives might be provided to people to make them want to keep working on something or to lean toward a certain concept or value.

3. Whatever is the most pleasing to someone might make a true difference.

Happiness is often something that inspires cognitive psychology. People are more likely to feel motivated when they can make positive connections to the things that they want to do in their lives. Having such good connections helps with keeping any process or action moving forward in a healthy and controlled fashion.

This can be noticed the most through the art of arousal. When a person is aroused, that person has a striking desire to do things. That person's curiosity and fascination for something will start to increase and become a little more prevalent. This makes it easier for someone to want to keep on working and doing things even if they are rather difficult to handle in some cases.

4. Everyone will be motivated based on their perceptions of what they find.

Cognitive psychology states that performance is dictated by how people see things. Those who find certain concepts or values to be worth more to them will want to work a little harder to complete the tasks they are asked to complete. When something does not have as much value attached to it, that person will not have a need to do it.

The next couple of chapters are devoted to various theories and concepts of cognitive motivation. These are points that can directly impact how well people might act and what they can get out of their lives.

Chapter 15 – Intrinsic Motivation

The next two chapters are dedicated to very important specific parts of motivation that must be explored in detail – intrinsic and extrinsic motivation. These parts of cognitive psychology focus on the connections that people have and how they might be developed. Let's look at the first of these points.

Intrinsic motivation is a vital part of this aspect of psychology that focuses on how a person might be motivated to do things based on the internal rewards that one can receive from an action.

For instance, a person might be interested in learning about many aspects of psychology. He might want to read a book on it because he has an interest in the subject and wants to learn more. He feels a desire to enrich his mind and expand his horizons.

This is an example of intrinsic motivation. He is motivated to read something through the internal values that he holds. He knows that there is something intriguing about the book he is reading that makes him want to continue reading. By acquiring more knowledge after reading that book, he will feel happier about himself. The information he has gathered could be used in many ways.

All About Happiness

The main concept of intrinsic motivation is that it is about happiness. People who are intrinsically motivated are not concerned about health, money, or social status. They are more interested in just being happy in general. A person might feel happy about something or might just like to do something in particular.

Some external rewards may still be produced when a person is intrinsically motivated. These rewards include monetary gain or maybe the acquisition of other resources, but the person's happiness is the top priority. The outside rewards that come later are a bonus.

Creativity Is Vital

The human brain is always looking for ways to evolve and learn new things. This includes knowing how to find new ideas or values that might make a difference in how one lives life. The creativity can through one's work and could be extensive and powerful. Creativity is a necessity for knowing what one can do for getting the most out of the work one might have to complete.

An intriguing part of the intrinsic motivation is that a person who is motivated in this way might feel creative. When a person does not think too much about money or other things, it becomes easier for that person to be more flexible. The person might want to find new ways to work and attain certain goals. It is all about making it easier for people to want to do what they feel is right and worthwhile in their lives.

The creative nature of one's work at this point might also be a sign of general enthusiasm and happiness. A person will want to keep on working just to see if certain things work out right. The happiness that one feels by learning something new or doing certain tasks will add to the motivation.

A person should be encouraged to be creative. This includes encouraging someone to find many solutions or interesting ideas to accomplish the tasks of one's work.

Overjustification

People might try to offer rewards to those who are intrinsically motivated. A business might tell someone who is already happy that they could get a monetary bonus for completing a certain task in a given time. However, the external rewards might make a task less intrinsically rewarding. This results in what is referred to as the overjustification effect.

At this point, a person will start to lose one's overall motivation to complete a task. The person becomes confused or conflicted as to what the true reward of something might be. A person might feel motivated to receive money, but at the same time, the enjoyment of the task will be lost because they are now just thinking about the money that could be earned.

The best thing that anyone in a workplace or school can do is to avoid trying to create something overly elaborate. It is important to fully understand the signs of intrinsic motivation.

Signs a Person Is Intrinsically Motivated

Workplaces that want to harness the power of intrinsically motivated employees will have to look at the many signs that suggest that someone is motivated in that way. In order to target a person who is intrinsically motivated, it is necessary to discover what makes that person tick or act in a particular way.

1. They display a strong interest in any task.

The thrill of doing a task or of learning something new and expanding one's horizons is often enough motivation. The thrill of doing things might be its own reward because of how diverse certain tasks or actions might be.

2. They are reflective.

Those who are reflective and think more about what they are doing in their lives will be intrinsically motivated. They will feel confident in what they are doing while knowing that they are always finding ways to learn new things.

3. They do not hold other people responsible for certain issues.

An intrinsic person always knows that it is one's own mind and actions that will directly impact what the person does at a given time. Those who are willing to work on their own and do their own thinking are intrinsically motivated. They know the things others in the workplace do are not necessarily going to contribute or affect their own work.

4. They interpret obstacles as challenges.

The opportunity of trying something new or different from the status quo is something that many intrinsically motivated people often find interesting and worthwhile. People who are intrinsically motivated will not be afraid of new things and the obstacles that may be involved. They will feel ready to get to work and will be excited to see what might happen.

5. They focus more on what they love.

Actions are always based on self-pleasure and interest. People who are thoughtful and concerned about what they can do in their lives are more likely to be intrinsically motivated. To them, work is less a chore and they are achievers and want to make a positive impact on the lives of other people.

6. They focus more on growth.

Motivated people are often willing to think more about how they can change their lives for the better. This includes wanting to learn more and do more at work and in their personal life.

How to Cater to Intrinsically Motivated People

After a business or school identifies someone as being intrinsically motivated, it should be easy to discover what can help improve that person's performance. There are many things that can be done to help those who are intrinsically motivated get the most out of the work that they want to complete:

1. Allow for more challenges.

Intrinsically motivated people love the challenges they are given. They see them as great learning opportunities. Businesses and schools need not worry if something is too difficult because an intrinsically motivated person will find a way to meet the challenge. All they need to complete a task is the resources they might require. Of course, the challenging task should be realistic.

2. Create something that piques one's curiosity.

Curiosity can be useful when dealing with those who are intrinsically motivated. A person's motivation will increase when something is introduced that grabs their attention and might cause them to want to learn something new.

3. Allow the person to have some control.

The creative and free-flowing nature of the intrinsic mind is critical to understand. Giving a person who thinks this way extra control over what they are doing without lots of rules or restrictions is something that will increase productivity.

4. Give a person the opportunity to help others.

People who think this way are willing to help others. The ability to assist other people in some way may be its own reward to those who really want to make a difference in the lives of other people.

5. Recognize their efforts.

The internal motivation that one has can be enhanced when their actions are recognized. They will notice that people are appreciative of what they are doing and they will feel rewarded for their efforts without any other incentive.

The art of intrinsic motivation is a valuable point for all to follow. Those who are identified as being intrinsically motivated are ones who are more likely to feel confident in their work and will complete certain tasks for the sake of it.

Chapter 16 – Extrinsic Motivation

Whereas intrinsic motivation focuses on understanding how people engage in tasks because they are rewarding in their own right, extrinsic motivation is the opposite direction. In this case, a person will participate in some action because that person knows there is a reward associated with it.

Extrinsic motivation relies on a person being motivated by a reward that is connected to a task. This connection involves a person wanting to work toward a particular goal when that goal is clearly and specifically defined.

For instance, a student in high school will want to keep on studying and completing her homework while working on tasks with classmates. She will do this with the knowledge that she could get a better grade in her class if she works hard.

Meanwhile, an athlete might participate in a sport because he wants to be recognized for his achievements. He will be working toward an award, a championship, and maybe even a sponsorship so that he can continue in his sport.

These two people are great examples of how extrinsic motivation works. This is a form of motivation where people are inspired to act in a certain way because they want a reward. The end result is different for each person.

In other cases, a person might initiate an action in order to avoid a negative outcome. The student might study and work hard on her assignments because she doesn't want a poor grade and therefore possibly miss out on a special honor or scholarship.

Satisfaction is not a factor in extrinsic motivation. It is all about simply working on ways to receive a reward for their efforts.

In fact, people who are extrinsically motivated will not always find enjoyment in the things that they do. They might simply do it because they know they will get something in return. For instance, a person might not be excited about getting to work each day, but that person will continue showing up anyway because that person knows there is a payment to be received. That person feels the situation will only get worse if they do not show up to work.

Rewards

Extrinsic motivation involves two kinds of rewards:

1. Tangible rewards

Tangible rewards might include money or special gifts. An athlete might compete to get a special trophy or a medal. A person could go out to a mining field in the hopes of finding diamonds or minerals that might be traded for money.

2. Psychological rewards

The psychological rewards that a person might earn include things like praise from a manager or a special public honor. Sometimes a child might clean one's room to hear positive things from a parent or just to keep that parent from getting frustrated or angry.

While intrinsic motivation involves people feeling motivated based on their individual desires, extrinsic motivation involves something outside that is a little more direct and unique. Managing these rewards can make a difference in motivating others.

Signs That Someone Is Extrinsically Motivated

While it is easy for businesses to notice when its employees are intrinsically motivated, it might be a little harder to see when someone is extrinsically motivated. There are a few signs of a person who is extrinsically motivated:

1. That person might not be interested in being around others.

An extrinsically motivated person might be very focused on the tasks and not on others around him. Every person has their own specific influences for completing certain tasks.

2. A person is punctual and not interested in social camaraderie.

While an intrinsically motivated person might want to do many things and engage in activities that are fun to do, an extrinsically motivated person will not be very flexible. That person might think more about doing things by the book or with a certain process in mind. It is a sign that someone is just doing things to get rewards for doing it right.

This is the opposite of intrinsic motivation; they would have a more freeform approach to work. The freedoms that come with extrinsic motivation are minimal and this could be useful in cases where an extremely specific pattern of work or a long list of rules have to be followed. Being able to work according to strict demands could be an asset.

A person could also have a hard time working alongside others in the same workplace.

It could be easy for certain people to have disputes with others because of certain differences. An extrinsically motivated person might not have the same bright attitude toward work as intrinsically motivated workers. This makes it all the more important for a manager to look at how people some people work better alone and some work better when paired with like-minded workers. This encourages harmony in the workplace.

Can Extrinsic Motivation Fail?

The main thing that businesses often do when helping people who are extrinsically motivated is to provide them with extra money, special raises or bonuses, or even special gifts or resources like a company car. However, there is potential for a person who is extrinsically motivated to suffer from the overjustification effect.

When that person receives a lot of rewards from a task, they might notice that the challenges are too easy. This makes it harder for a person to feel motivated to keep working. The person thinks that the rewards will continue and they lose the incentive to work hard.

This is illustrated by a famous experiment conducted by M.R. Lepper and two others in 1973. They gave rewards to children who engaged in drawing activities on their own time. When the children were given the opportunity to voluntarily continue drawing, the children declined. This suggests that those who are extrinsically motivated, such as continue to draw, will want to continue, but it might be harder for them to do this when they notice that they are being recognized.

This does not mean that absolutely no recognition or reward should be given. A person can still be subjected to some recognition and reward for the duties that they do.

Best When a Person Shows Struggles To Do Something

The best way to address a person who is extrinsically motivated is to look at how that person reacts to a certain task. A person might feel that they are unable to complete a task or might not have much interest for whatever reason. Offering a special reward to that person will help entice them to want to do something and try one's hand at a special activity. This is a simple offer that improves upon one's chances for success.

A person who is extrinsically motivated should not be considered as someone to avoid. If anything, such a person might be proficient in their work and continue to work hard. It might be difficult for them to feel encouraged to do things at certain times if they feel as though they are forced to perform certain tasks.

How Long Should a Person Be Extrinsically Motivated?

Although it is easy to work alongside those who are extrinsically motivated, it is vital to watch for how long it takes for such a person to go from being motivated to not being willing to perform. As a person continues to work on a certain job for a long time, they may begin to feel worn out. There might be less incentive for someone to do things based on factors like money or other rewards. That person might feel that they have enough money and, therefore, is not going to be as motivated.

There might also be times when someone begins to get bored with the same routines and that boredom comes from actions being repetitive or nothing new ever being introduced. When this happens, motivation lessens.

It might be helpful to encourage someone to become intrinsically motivated. This might include allowing a person to be more creative in the job. Perhaps new experiences can be introduced including new people or new responsibilities are required. This will broaden their horizons and move from extrinsic motivations and closer to an intrinsic motivation.

The amount of time it takes for someone to become jaded by extrinsic motivation will vary. Someone could remain motivated extrinsically for years before their performance starts to decline. The best thing for a business or school to do is to look at how that person's performance standards are changing and if that person is not achieving the success that they had in the past. There might be a need to change things for them by introducing more intrinsic values into the workplace or school to allow someone to stay productive or confident in their ability to work.

Chapter 17 – Arousal Theory

When people think about the term "arousal," they think about how a person will develop a sudden sense of pleasure about certain things. People typically think that arousal involves sexual satisfaction. The arousal theory is about more than just sexual pleasure. It is about pleasure for practically anything that a person might do. Sex is just a small part of it all.

Arousal theory is a part of the motivation that links to the drive-reduction theory. The drive-reduction theory concentrates on the desire that a person has to resolve certain drives. The arousal theory is about satisfaction and focuses on a particular neurotransmitter in the brain.

The Value of Dopamine

For the arousal theory to work, the brain will require a vital compound for it to stay active. This compound is known as dopamine.

Dopamine is a critical neurotransmitter that determines how well the brain functions. It controls how the brain identifies rewards and pleasure. It also influences the emotional responses. When the brain gets enough dopamine, it becomes easier for a person to stay motivated and take action to complete certain tasks.

Dopamine moves between neurons in the brains to trigger feelings of satisfaction and motivation. It is what prompts people to continue to engage in certain behaviors when they notice that there are some benefits associated with those behaviors.

The brain needs enough dopamine to manage a sense of motivation. A person who does not have enough dopamine in their brain might struggle with being motivated as they do not recognize the proper motivation that directly impacts certain actions or attitudes.

Those who have too much dopamine in the brain will develop addictions to certain pleasure-associated behaviors. This can be very problematic when it comes to illegal drug use. Some illegal drugs might cause significant spikes in dopamine levels, thus making it harder for that person to want to stop using a drug.

Dopamine is often produced through various medications. Drugs like ropinirole and pramipexole may be used to help people restore their mental functions by having more dopamine produced within the brain. However, the prescriptions might cause too much of the transmitter to be produced, thus leading to impulsive and potentially dangerous behaviors. Therefore, medications are often used as a last resort to help manage this chemical.

A better way to manage a person's dopamine is to see if that person might respond to certain concepts or actions. As this chapter will explain, it might be easy to influence one's arousal by considering how a person's attitudes might be directly influenced in some way.

Every Person Has a Different Arousal Level

The arousal theory of motivation is based on how a person can feel encouraged. When a person is aroused by something, it becomes easier for that person to continue working toward a certain goal.

Everyone has a unique arousal level. Every person is different in that they will have their own particular reasons for what they feel is valuable. Sometimes the production of dopamine in the brain might make an impact as it triggers what someone might be interested in.

The arousal theory states that a person's arousal levels will directly impact their motivation. For instance, a person might become aroused and entertained when he is hanging out with his friends. He will feel happy and will be motivated to do things with his friends.

However, that person might get into a situation where he is too aroused. He might feel too energetic and could be less motivated after a while to engage in certain actions. He might want to slow down or doing something else that is relaxing and comforting.

This is an interesting point of the arousal theory in that a person can only get so excited. A proper balance has to be used to where a person will feel motivated toward feeling great but will need to work in moderation to keep from becoming tired.

Here is a better example of how this works. A man might be traveling in Las Vegas and will want to enjoy the nightlife and all the things the city's casinos have to offer. When he gets on the casino floor, he will begin to feel aroused. He will be excited by the variety of games on the floor and the many experiences in such a place. After a while, that arousal will become too intense. He might not feel very motivated after spending too much time on the casino floor. He might be tired of the games or he could be frustrated because he is not winning the games. Whatever the case might be, he could g back to his hotel room to rest before he continues enjoying himself.

In terms of dopamine, there is a chance that a person will respond to certain things differently based on the amount of this chemical produced within the brain. Those who get enough dopamine in their brains are likely to feel motivated and encouraged to stay productive.

Can Arousal Impact Performance? (The Yerkes-Dodson Law)

One interesting part of the arousal theory that many people, particularly those who run businesses, consider is how it can influence how a person performs. The levels of arousal that someone has could make a real difference in performance, but at some point, they may be too aroused and then performance will be negatively affected.

The Yerkes-Dodson Law states that a person who experiences a strong level of arousal will start to perform well. That person will keep working hard and will feel motivated to keep up a strong effort. However, after a while, that person will reach their maximum level of arousal. This causes the person to start to feel tired and less likely to want to keep working. That person's performance (in both speed and quality) will start to decline at this juncture.

The law also says that a person's level of arousal will make an even bigger impact when a task being completed is more complicated. Those who are handling many tasks at a time and are putting in more effort into the overall process will feel greater benefits by being aroused during a task. Meanwhile, a tough project will be significantly harder for someone to finish when that person is no longer feeling as excited as one wished.

A great example is when a student might try to pass a series of final exams in high school. A student will feel more motivated to keep working on exams and to study when they are aroused. They will feel excited about working hard, but after a while, all that arousal will make it harder for them to keep on studying. Even worse, that student might struggle with anxiety before a test and might feel worn out from all the studying.

In short, the Yerkes-Dodson Law can be illustrated by an inverted-U in terms of one's arousal level and performance:

1. A person's arousal level will be low at the start while one's performance is weak.

2. After a while, the interest and arousal in something will increase so that person is going to keep on working hard.

3. All that arousal can lead to anxiety or fatigue over time, thus making a person feel tired and incapable of producing as well as one did in the past.

Schools and businesses can use the Yerkes-Dodson Law to identify how well people are performing by comparing one's results with the general attitudes a person holds when doing something. The general goal is to keep a person from continuing certain behaviors that might be too hard.

What Will Influence the Law?
The Yerkes-Dodson Law will be influenced by four things. These relate to how well a person is capable of doing things.

1. How complicated a task is

It is more difficult for a person to become aroused when a task is hard. They have the feeling that they are being tested and that the things they are being asked to do are too complicated or hard to figure out.

2. Ability level

A person's ability to complete a task can directly influence their motivation. A person who is skilled at a certain task and understands how to complete it will feel more confident in their ability to finish the task. Those who know what they are doing will not have to work too hard to become aroused. To an experienced person, a certain task might be like second nature. This works well if that person is ready for the task at hand and is not afraid of what might happen. It might take months or years for a person's ability level to grow to the point where they will not struggle when trying to complete certain tasks.

3. Personality

One's personality is an important element. An extroverted person might feel more motivated because they feel confident with certain tasks. The pleasure that comes from working might be higher because they are ready to show off their abilities. Introverted people might feel confident in how they can work, but they are typically focused more on their own benefits. They might be more intrinsic based on what they want to do.

4. How confident a person is in one's abilities

Even those who are capable of working hard and producing the best results on any project might still feel pressure. Some people will feel uncertain as to whether or not they can take care of tasks the right way. A person might have the ability to write a massive book, but he or she might feel nervous and unsure of finishing the project.

Those who are trained for longer periods of time will feel more confident in what they can do. These include people who have studied something for months or years and might have had some hands-on experience with the task at hand. The confidence that a person has will directly influence how they complete tasks.

What Is the Proper Arousal Level?

The Yerkes-Dodson Law is helpful to understand how arousal works. While this law has been used by many since the early 20th Century, it is still impossible to determine the threshold of a person when aroused. Every person, particularly in a school or work setting, has their own standards for working. Some people are likely to be excited about working or studying but could quickly lose motive.

A good thing to do is to take a careful look at how individual students or employees work throughout a period of time. A manager or teacher can look at how well people are performing over a period and then see if there is a drop in production. There will be a drop that suggests a point at which person is not as aroused by their work as they used to be.

It is clear that the arousal levels are going to be impacted more when the task is complex. The threshold level of arousal might be higher when the task is more difficult to complete. For instance, it is very easy for a person to feel motivated when taking a shower or doing some other task or habit that does not require mental or physical effort. The arousal level might need to be higher when working on a paper project. It could be harder for a person to feel motivated to get started on something, but after a while, it will become easier to get into a groove and really start to work on something.

There is one problem to consider. Although people can observe others to see how aroused they are, it would be impossible to determine who is the most motivated at any time. There is no way to measure someone's attitudes and behaviors. Although dopamine is clearly a part of arousal, it is a challenge to determine how much of that chemical a person is producing. Only estimates can be made, thus leading to the need to determine if someone needs medication or if further observation or emotional support might be required to keep a person active.

Chapter 18 – The Incentive Theory

People love to receive rewards for the things that they do. They love it when they get bonuses at work for the things that they have been doing. Students love to get extra credit when they show certain attributes or skills that are above and beyond what they are expected to do. Simply put, incentives are often given to help people work to their best abilities and to get more out of the work they are putting in.

Incentives and rewards have become an everyday part of life. Everyone loves rewards; practically everyone is offering rewards for jobs done. Credit card companies offer reward points for purchases, air travel service providers give people frequent flyer miles as rewards to use for free travel in the future.

People who are provided with appealing incentives believe they will receive something of value. Some might think this theory of motivation is just a psychological concept that is bribing people to do things.

The incentive theory has been used by psychologists since the mid-20th Century as a practice that can help people identify what they can do at a given point. The concept states that people will be motivated based on certain goals that are presented to them. These include special goals where a person who does a certain task or engages in a particular behavior will be given something in return. Regardless of what that reward is, there is always a good chance that the reward will be seen as something positive.

How This Works

The incentive theory is based on outside stimuli. In this case, it is the reward that a person will receive that motivates a person to do something. All that matters at this juncture is that a person knows what will happen when that person performs a certain activity. It is up to the person being offered a reward to determine if that reward is enough of a motivating factor.

The practice uses a few basic steps:

1. A person is told to do something or act in some way.

2. That person is being presented with a special reward for engaging in a specific behavior.

3. That person would then begin that particular behavior.

4. The reward will be given to the person based on how well they follow the instructions.

This could be interpreted as a form of operant conditioning. Operant conditioning occurs when a person performs certain actions as a means of gaining some kind of reinforcement or possibly to avoid a punishment.

There is a major difference between operant conditioning and the incentive theory. In operant conditioning, people are led into automatically or instinctually engaging in certain actions based on positive or negative stimuli. With the incentive theory, a person will be rewarded based on the actions that someone might legitimately engage in.

Here is an example. A grocery store might encourage people to sign up for a special shopping card to receive special discounts on groceries. Such a card would collect the customer's information, particularly their contact data and information on how someone spends money on groceries. The store would encourage a person to sign up for the card by offering many types of incentives. A person can not only get special discounts on the groceries but also rewards for special gifts and items that the store might offer. This is provided to allow the store to compete with other grocery outlets in an already saturated market.

The rewards that someone is given will encourage that person to sign up for such a card. That person can then use the card at a particular store to have access to various exclusive discounts on products. The reward, in this case, will be savings on one's order. Sometimes the reward will expand to include things like free cutlery sets, free patio furniture, discounts at gas stations, and so forth.

The incentive theory works as the customer is willing to provide their information to the grocery store chain in exchange for special rewards and discounts. The customer will not question why the store needs their information. Rather, that customer will simply go to the store to buy things and receive the discounts.

Making Things Pleasant

The most commonplace reason why rewards are given is so that people will feel interested in doing things that they might normally have very little interest in doing. It is difficult, and maybe impossible, for people to do their chores or to go to work if they do not feel that they are going to get rewards from that work. When a good reward is offered, it becomes easier for someone to be convinced to want to do some work.

It becomes easier and potentially more enjoyable for people to engage in actions when they feel that there is a positive benefit to be realized. Retail stores often provide rewards to people who spend money on certain things to make it easier for those people to want to spend their money. People might be more willing to do this when they see that they will get more out of a purchase.

In the case of the grocery store, the store is making it easier for people to enjoy buying groceries. People will start to notice that there are many good deals in the store. They might even be guided toward products based on the discounts available. Of course, there is a chance that a person might spend more money than they planned simply because they might find lots of deals on products they might not have thought about.

Even if more money is spent, the customer will feel happy. They will feel as though they got a great deal on a shopping trip because of the things that were on sale.

Common Types of Rewards

There are no rules as to what types of rewards can be offered. Money is clearly the most popular reward. People often go to their jobs not so much to have something to do but rather to simply make money. When a person is motivated by money, it becomes easier for that person to work and to stay positive.

Sometimes the rewards in the workplace can be more than just money. A person might also receive a special award or maybe some unique bonus offered by a company. This could include added vacation time or time off with pay. Without the possibility of a reward, it becomes harder for a person to want to keep on working.

Students might be motivated to study and do well with their homework in order to have good grades as the reward. Students might also feel motivated by the potential to gain respect from other students and their teachers if they get the best grades possible.

There has to be some kind of tangible or emotional value attached to the reward. When the value is strong, people will want to work harder and do better.

Getting Away from Negative Events

An interesting psychological part of the incentive theory is that it focuses on how people might be encouraged to engage in certain actions based on what they find to be valuable. More importantly, people might begin to notice that not engaging in activities that do not have any rewards might cause some negative issues.

What is even more intriguing is that a person who ignores or refuses to engage in negative events might not even be aware of how negative those issues are. In order to engage in a negative event, the reward is the only thing that the person would be thinking about.

In the grocery store example, the reward cards that a store might offer will help people feel confident and think they are likely to save money. The store might explain that by using the cards that are available to them, they will avoid the problems associated with missing out on certain offers. Sometimes the discounts being offered on certain items might be significant and make products people normally cannot afford easier to purchase.

FOMO Issues

The incentive theory particularly focuses on FOMO issues. This refers to the "fear of missing out." The theory allows businesses to market items or services that people need to purchase right now. People are motivated to by knowing that certain offers or events might only last for a limited time. This triggers a fear in some people that they will miss out on something special if they delay purchasing it. When that person misses out on something, that person will feel unhappy because they were unable to participate in something before the savings were discontinued.

Missing out on something big is one of the most prominent negative events that people often try to avoid. When someone sees that a huge event is happening for a limited time, that person will want to take advantage of it. People might not be motivated to do things, but will end up wanting to do them if they see there is an extremely limited amount of time associated with the purchase.

Businesses can benefit from this as they might post openings for new positions but that the opening will only be available for a few days. This would cause people who are interested to apply as quickly as possible before time runs out. If the position was open-ended, people might not be in a rush to sign up or apply. With time constraints attached to it, it is an incentive for people to act.

Can Rewards Help People Stop Behaving In a Certain Way?

One other part of the incentive theory of motivation involves how a person might be motivated to stop doing certain things. Although most people might assume that the incentive theory focuses more on getting people to engage in certain actions, it might also help people to learn how to stop doing certain things. For instance, a person might be given the opportunity to do something special at one's job if that person stops working on a certain task.

One example is how a business might encourage anyone who smokes to stop doing so. A business could reward smokers who aim to stop smoking a special reward like a special insurance package or some added access to certain health-related services that a business offers to its employees for free. By giving a person the ability to access certain things, it might be easier for someone to stop a bad habit.

This application of the incentive theory is not used as often as other solutions.

Everything Has to Be Obtainable

The incentive theory would be worthless if a reward is impossible for a person to reach. There has to be a sense of realism in the task so that someone will actually feel motivated. When a task is perceived as being too difficult, it becomes harder for a person to want to complete that task.

An example of this might be being required to complete a paper on a particular subject that is a few thousand words long. A paper might be due in a few days and could be easy for someone to complete when they have done a similar paper the past. However, it would be impossible for a person to feel motivated when they believe that the task in question is impossible to finish. For instance, a person who needs to complete a task that big might be told to finish it within 24 hours. That person might not be motivated at this point because it would be impossible to actually finish that task within that brief time.

The type of reward would have to be even greater depending on the situation. If a person has to finish that paper in a shorter period of time, they will expect a greater reward, such as a better grade or be given extra credit. If that person does not get the reward that one is expecting, they will be reluctant or refuse to engage in the activity.

The grocery store reward card offered rewards that might be easily obtainable; a person just has to go into a store, pick up an item, swipe the card at the check-out, and then pay the discounted price. There might also be cases where the card offers a reward that might be unrealistic. A store might offer a free outdoor patio furniture set that would normally cost a few hundred dollars. However, to get that set, a customer would have to spend an unreasonable amount of money on groceries for a few weeks, and this may discourage the customer. They might not find the incentive to be worthwhile due to the belief that it would be very difficult to get that reward.

Negative Incentives

While incentives are typically associated with being positive, they can also be negative. A negative incentive is one that is given when a person does not complete a certain action or refuses to do a task. An example of this is when a student does not complete their homework on time. That student might be scolded by the teacher and get a lower grade. This is a negative incentive that the student would be motivated to avoid.

Negative incentives are often used to motivate people by making them realize that there are certain things that they should avoid doing at all costs. These incentives help correct a person's behavior. A person would just be encouraged to avoid certain actions before they can become more difficult.

An even better example is how a credit card company treats its customers. A company will ask its customers to pay their bills on time. The negative incentive, in this case, would be added charges like a late fee for not paying the minimum payment or greater on time. Added interest charges might also be incurred with those costs making things even more expensive.

The charges could add up over time if they are not handled. This negative incentive is offered by credit card companies to ensure that people will pay their bills on time.

The overall point about the incentive theory is that it focuses on making it easier for people to want to accomplish tasks. People who might be told to engage in particular actions in exchange for special rewards are often going to want to comply.

Chapter 19 – Expectancy Theory

The expectancy theory is a motivational theory that was developed by psychologist Victor Vroom in 1964 as a means of looking at what causes motivation to develop.

The basic concept of the expectancy theory is that a person who follows the theory is going to expect rewards that relate directly to how well a person performs. The rewards in question are expected to be the ones that the person might want more than anything else.

The general goal is to maximize the overall pleasure that one gets from work. When a person follows the expectancy theory, they will be motivated to work with the assumption that something is going to come about and that the end result will be favorable and worthwhile.

Four Key Factors

There are four vital factors of the expectancy theory:

1. There must be a positive connection between effort and performance.

In this case, a person who puts in more effort into any task will be more likely to succeed. This could be used by managers to recognize how important it is for people to work harder and those who put in the best efforts will do the most. Those who know what to expect if they work hard and do their best will want to keep on working.

2. The best performances will result in rewards.

Those who do the most will be rewarded. A person who works harder than others in a business environment is likely to receive extra pay, a bonus or at least be considered for more hours of work, thus resulting in a higher pay. An athlete will expect to receive a special medal or trophy for physically out-performing others in a sport.

3. The rewards that are given will satisfy a certain need.

The needs will vary based on each person who participates. A person might get money that will satisfy one's need for paying off a mortgage or apartment rent. An athlete would get an award for their performance. Such an honor would satisfy the need to feel accomplished and would prove that their work to become the best possible athlete was worthwhile.

4. The motivation to satisfy a need must be strong enough so that the effort being put into the action is worthwhile.

A person might be motivated to earn money or to get recognition. When that person is motivated, it becomes easier for them to want to do things and to be more active in trying to attain certain goals or standards.

Although every person has their own skill sets and desires, they may be motivated in accordance with the expectancy theory if they notice that there is something good that will come as a result of effort. This works best for those who put in the greatest amount of effort into producing more work.

Valence

There are three critical beliefs about how the expectancy theory of motivation works. First, there is the belief of valence. It relates to the emotional needs that people have toward certain things that might happen. Specifically, it is about how a person might feel based on what could happen and if there is a problem with a certain outcome. Some people might be more motivated to do things because they fear a certain outcome more than they want a favorable outcome.

The valence in the situation does not refer to the value that a person places on the reward. Rather, it is about the level of satisfaction as a result of a certain outcome. A person's needs, goals, and preferences for what may happen are vital to the success. A person might welcome an outcome when certain things are done and will, therefore, want to move forward toward attaining that outcome.

For example, a person might notice that he could earn money by working on a certain task that is voluntary in the workplace. He might also choose to reject the optional task but would not earn the money. He might value the money enough so that he would not like the outcome of missing out on an opportunity for money. Therefore, he would take on that optional task because he will still be pleased with the outcome of the project.

A business will have to identify what individual employees value the most when looking at what causes people to act in certain ways. This includes determining how people might respond to certain stimuli or be inspired to act in specific ways based on what they expect to get out of an event.

In short, a person must prefer having certain outcome rather than not getting it. In the example above, the worker might recognize that the optional task he has to complete would require extra work over time, but he would be willing to work on it because he knows that the outcome of getting extra money is worthwhile to him. He values money more than someone else in the workplace might. Each individual person will feel motivated in a different way to choose to either accept or reject a particular activity.

Three Vital Numbers

The best way to understand the valence of the expectancy theory is to utilize three numbers. These are reflective of the attitudes one holds:

-1: Someone wants to avoid a specific outcome.

0: There are no concerns over the results.

+1: A person wants an outcome in a certain way.

A good way to measure one's desires is to ask that person about all the outcomes that might be possible. A person's answers can be tallied based on how badly someone wants a certain thing to happen. All of the answers can be added together to decide if someone wants to have a certain result when working in some way. A higher positive score always means that a person wants to keep on working.

Expectancy

The second part of the theory to look into involves expectancy. This refers to how a person believes that by putting in a certain effort, they will reach particular performance goals. An employee might have a certain expectation as to what one has to do while also feeling confident about what can be done in the workplace.

The expectancy aspect of the expectancy theory is often based on prior experiences of that worker. For instance, a worker might have had to work at a retail store during a major holiday. She might have recalled that the store was busier during that time, but she would have also received extra pay because the store had a higher pay schedule for holidays.

However, she might also notice that the task will be difficult. She expects it to be harder because she would be dealing with a larger volume of customers with many of them being customers who are unfamiliar with how a certain store operates.

Her confidence in the ability to complete a task is also important. She might feel motivated to work because she knows she is capable of handling the task. If she is not confident, she might not be motivated to actually move toward engaging in certain actions.

There are three aspects of the expectancy concept:

1. Self-efficacy

Self-efficacy is how well a person might be able to perform an action. Those who have the skills needed to complete a task will feel motivated and positive.

2. Goal Difficulty

The goals or expectations that a person has might be perceived as being just right to some people. Someone might feel comfortable to keep working on a certain task, thus creating a higher level of expectancy for completing a task. When the task appears to be too hard, that person is not going to be as motivated due to the belief that the goals are impossible to attain.

3. Control

A person must feel that they have some kind of control over a task. A person should know how to control the situation to make it work in their favor. A person who sees a task as being impossible to manipulate or control will not feel motivated. That person might think that the task is impossible and that the lack of flexibility will deter them from attaining a certain goal.

This part of the expectancy theory is important because a person might believe that the effort required will result in better performance and therefore a greater reward. Employers will have to determine how individual people think about certain concepts.

Instrumentality

The third part of the expectancy theory focuses on instrumentality. This concentrates on the promises being made and if they might be kept. An employee might feel that they will receive what they are expecting, but it is up to the manager to promise it. When a person believes in what the manager is saying that person becomes motivated because of the expectation of the reward actually being given.

The rewards that a person might expect could involve a pay raise, a promotion, or some simple recognition of the work done.

Instrumentality levels are high when people know that the rewards and outcomes are different. For instance, a track and field athlete who wants to compete in the Olympics will anticipate winning a medal and receiving added recognition if he does his best and performs better than others in his sport. His instrumentality level will be high because he knows that a specific reward or special benefit will happen.

On the other hand, the instrumentality level will decline when it is seen that the reward level is the same for all people who participate. The athlete will not feel encouraged to compete if he notices that everyone will get the same reward for competing in a track and field event. He would be much more motivated if he knew that he would get a better reward if there were multiple outcomes and different rewards for participation.

Three factors will have to be reviewed:

1. A person must trust someone who is offering rewards based on the performances.

2. There has to be some control over how decisions are made and how people are to be rewarded. This includes specific parameters that determine which outcomes will be rewarded to specific groups of people.

3. There must be some sensible policies that link a performance and the outcome. A policy could include a definition of what has to be accomplished for someone to reach a particular result.

Workplaces can use this part of the motivation to change how they might work. There has to be a way to guarantee particular rewards based on performances. This could not only create a more productive workplace where people will perform to reach certain outcomes but also a more competitive workplace. The competition between people will cause them to work to their best abilities so they can merit the rewards.

What is even more important is that a manager knows how to satisfy the desires that people have. The manager has to manage the resources and provide the motivation needed to give the workers the rewards that they are expecting. When those rewards are given to people, it becomes easier for them to stay motivated. They know they can expect to be paid based on the work accomplished.

What Is the Final Motivational Force?

All three parts of this theory combine into what is known as the motivational force. The expectancy that someone holds, the valence associated, and the instrumentality combines into a single profile. An employee, student or another person can be consulted and questions about possible outcomes, the effort that would be required to attain certain outcomes and the consequences if the effort is not strong or effective.

A person's motivation will be greater when all three of these variables have higher ratings. The variables will show that someone is willing to keep working toward a goal. Knowing how to target people based on their values and beliefs can make a difference.

Chapter 20 – Equity Theory

A sense of balance is a necessity to have in one's life. When there is a sense of equity in the workplace, people to feel confident and capable of doing more because there is a balance between the effort made and the reward that is given. That reward will be worthless if the worker feels too much effort is required.

The equity theory is a concept that states that a person will only be motivated based on the fairness of the task.

How This Works

The equity theory depends on:

1. A worker looks at the job according to the effort needed.

The input refers to the contribution someone might bring to a task. For instance, a basketball player might notice that he needs to put in a strong physical effort into what he is doing. He might be asked to be the leader of a team or maybe just a role player who functions as a specific member of the team.

2. The outcome that results from completing the task can be analyzed.

The outcome refers to how someone will be compensated. It could involve money but sometimes it is all about the experience. The basketball player in this example might feel that he is worth more than others because he puts in the greater effort. While getting an award or trophy or even some recognition for his efforts might be great, he could ask for more money than others on the team.

3. The first two points are compared with whatever someone else in the same category does.

The comparison helps to decide if that person is being given the same compensation for doing the same things that someone else might be doing. This is to see if the compensation for the same performance is identical.

The basketball player might compare the salary he receives with the salaries of other people on the team. He might be fine with being paid the most money if he is the team leader and is responsible for more things and for controlling a game. He might also compare other leaders of various teams and see that some of them might be receiving more compensation than he is. He might be upset because he feels he is not getting the money he thinks he rightfully deserves.

The output-into ratio can then be developed. One of three results will occur:

1. A person feels under-rewarded and is not receiving enough compensation.

2. There is a sense of equity where the compensation for one's performance is just right.

3. Someone might also be over-rewarded and is receiving too great a compensation for their efforts.

An employee might feel more motivated if there is a sense of equity or even if that person is getting over-rewarded. When that person feels under-rewarded it becomes a challenge to feel motivated. Proper corrective measures might be required including moving a person to a new position or expanding upon the compensation provided it is reasonable.

In most cases, the employee who feels under-rewarded will have their say as to what they can do. That person can try to increase one's workload or to improve upon their skills in the hopes of possibly getting more money. There is also the option to choose a different position within a group. A person could also leave a group and go where there is the potential to make more money.

What could help solve someone's issue is to have them change their perception. The basketball player in this example might have to change his attitudes if he notices he is not being compensated properly. He might begin to notice that his role is not as important as it used to be. He might also realize that maybe other people in his profession are just as valuable as he is and that he is placing too great a value on himself. By changing his attitudes, the chances for him to perform and feel motivated will increase as he no longer feels upset over the situation.

Moderating Variables

The moderating variables involved in this theory deserve some recognition. The equity theory states that several things might make a difference when looking at how someone is compensated.

1. Level of experience

The amount of experience that someone has in a field is often the most important point to consider. Those who are more experienced are more likely to succeed and advance in their line of work.

2. Education

People who are well-educated tend to be motivated because they know what to do in the workplace. They also expect to be paid more because of the perceived value of their expertise.

3. Salary

The perceptions people have about payments for services can directly influence what one will do in the workplace.

4. Gender

Men and women often have their own ideas for how they are to be compensated. Men often compare their salaries with what other men earn. However, women often have lower salary expectations than men. Men are often paid more than women in some positions, although there is always a potential for a woman to expect and demand to be paid the same as a man for the same work.

People are going to be motivated when they notice that they are being paid an appropriate amount of money for the work that they do. When people determine that they are being paid properly and adequately, they will have confidence in the work they are doing.

Chapter 21 – Goal-Setting Theory

The last point for cognitive psychology and motivation and performance to review involves how people will set their own goals. In the 1960s, Edwin Locke introduced a new theory relating to motivation that he called the goal-setting theory. This focuses on how goals inspire people to perform and work to their potential.

The goal-setting theory states that people are more likely to feel motivated when they are given specific and certain goals to attain. These include goals that might be harder to reach. Those who are given easy goals might not do as well. They might feel that they can cruise and not put much effort into a task. That lack of drive will result in a lower performance level, thus making it easier for a person to fail.

By supporting workers through the use of distinct goals, it becomes easy for those goals to be effective and for a business to move forward.

What Makes the Theory Special?

There are no limits when producing goals. The general objective is to allow people in the workplace to feel positive and to see that they are supported in their development and how they are treated fairly.

With the goal-setting theory, a business will use several points:

1. The goals that can be used must be as clear and specific as possible.

The key is to allow all people in the workplace to fully understand what they are supposed to do. This includes knowing what makes certain tasks important and how they can be completed.

2. All goals have to be challenging but at the same time able to be completed through reasonable effort.

People will enjoy accepting challenging goals if they have the belief that they are given greater rewards. Some people might not be motivated to do specific things because they feel that the goals are too difficult and the rewards too small.

3. The goals must be organized so that many people will work together to complete them.

The goals can be worthwhile if organized with many people in mind. A goal should be designed so that multiple people would be willing to work with one another to achieve an end result.

Important Points to Note

The goal-setting theory is a dynamic part of the motivation that could be effective in larger IT offices where people are told to work toward producing a larger database or connectivity structure for a client to use. It might also work when a grocery store needs to get some new displays set up or to help manage the inventory. There are a few things that must be followed regardless of the specific application:

1. The overall goal of the theory is to help people to work faster.

While motivation is important, the theory focuses on performance and productivity above all else. This theory works best in environments where there is a great amount of competition and challenges.

2. This can also be useful when a business needs to maintain a sense of teamwork.

The teamwork depends on people getting along with each other to attain the same types of goals.

3. The most difficult and complicated goals are always the ones that have the riskiest behaviors.

Although it is always good to create challenging goals, it is at important to be aware of how difficult they are. The goal-setting theory will backfire because the goals being produced are too elaborate or complicated.

4. The goals that are produced should be compared with what a manager wants to accomplish.

The goals that employees have might be different from what a manager wants to do. It is critical to be aware how the goals between employees and managers might clash or be at odds.

The overall point about the goal-setting theory is that the goals that people are given can help them be more productive.

Chapter 22 – Developmental Perspectives on Motivation

An amazing part of the human brain is that it is a truly untamed beast. While many people might assume that the brain is going to cause a person to act in one way throughout life, there is actually a greater likelihood that a person's brain will transform and change over time. The brain will evolve as the body grows. Brain cells will form and new connections will be established after a time. At the same time, the brain may atrophy over the years and have fewer connections that work as well as before.

People will have particular motivations that might change over the years. For instance, a child might not feel motivated to read while in school but she is only doing so because her class at school requires her to do it.

Over time, she may develop an interest in reading. She might choose to read things to learn more or simply because she is curious. She may start to read books that she wants to read on her own and eventually develop a positive habit of learning through various types of books. Her motivations may also change over time because she may want to read specific kinds of books about subjects she is interested in.

Developmental changes in a person's brain can cause that person to act differently and to be interested in certain concepts. The world of developmental psychology is extremely complicated. Having a better understanding of how the human brain evolves and changes over time is critical to know what to expect from certain people.

The developmental considerations may relate to understanding the psychology of adult workers. As the brain experiences new things and develops, various opinions can be eventually set in stone. It is up to managers to understand how to leverage the development of the individual worker so they can recognize what they can do and how they can grow as people.

Nature vs. Nurture

The first concept is the idea of nature vs. nurture. Developmental psychology is based on how it explains a person's mental capacity is formed. This can be divided up into two parts:

1. Nature

This is a belief that a person has innate traits and behaviors that might cause them to act in certain ways. The motivational factors are inherited from that person's parents. It is about heredity and genetics above all else in this case.

2. Nurture

This is the belief that a person's environment is responsible for determining how a person develops to have certain behaviors. That person is exposed to many outside factors that trigger how one is to be motivated.

Nature

Nature and nurture are important to motivation. First, there is nature. There are some parts of the human mind and body that will be determined genetically by heredity. One's hair color, body type, blood type, and the possibility of developing certain medical conditions are all parts of nature.

Some of the characteristics one has are not going to be visible at birth, but over time they will start to naturally develop. This includes the natural feelings of motivation that a person holds.

The nature philosophy believes that instincts are going to dictate many of the things that people do and believe. The innate drive might be influenced by genetics.

It would be extremely difficult for managers to change the natural ways a person's brain develops. Some hereditary characteristics will determine how a person acts. A manager has to identify what a person does and how that person is inspired to act. There is always the possibility of using a questionnaire or other test to analyze how someone will act, but that might still be difficult to analyze and predict future actions and behaviors.

Nurture

The experiences that a person has in life will influence how a person develops and what motivates them to act. The environment might feature many dramatic changes in one's life and can directly influence how they think and act.

For instance, a man might have been raised with his mother being very close to him throughout his life. He might have been protected by her over the years as she worked to provide for him. throughout his entire life. The nurture concept of motivation suggests that he will be motivated more by his mother than anything. While he might not feel motivated to do certain things in his life when she is not involved, he might be encouraged even further to do something if he notices that his mother or someone else close to him is in danger or could be impacted in some way.

It is through this that one's ability to handle certain ideas might be impacted. When a person is nurtured in some fashion, that person will have a predisposition to focus on certain concepts. A person might be more motivated to support certain ideas because one's parents did. The direct impact of the things a person is surrounded by over time will make a major impact on their levels of motivation.

A business could use the nurturing part of the brain's development by exposing a new worker to not only the basic things he needs to know at the start but also the concepts that the business expects to use. During an orientation process, people might learn many things that are easy for them to recall like the history of a business, its main principles, the general tasks and jobs that people do, any resources that may be used while on the job and so forth. This is to create a better understanding of the many things that someone can do while working. The new workers will be nurtured into wanting to work for a company and fully understanding the how that business works.

The Development of the Senses

One part of developmental psychology is how a child's senses are formed. Motivation can develop even at a very young age. People are often motivated by their senses. A person will not want to eat something that person does not like if the food produces negative sensations. Meanwhile, some people might be turned off by certain scents and will want to avoid particular situations. Every person is different as to how their senses are formed; the best way to consider this is to look far back into a person's life to see what might cause someone to act in certain ways toward particular senses.

When a child is born, his or her body does not have all of its senses intact yet. It takes a period of time for a child's senses to develop so they can see things, touch items, and feel sensations. For instance, a child's sense of sight might start to develop while in the womb, it will not be fully developed until around six to eight months of age.

The senses help a child develop a sense of motivation. Let's say that the first thing that a child sees is his mother. He will become motivated when he sees her because he has developed a connection with his mother. The visual motivation of this child is the positive connection to his mother. This is something that could be relevant to adulthood. When a person starts a new job with a new employer, that person might latch on to the first things that he sees or does. He might be attached to certain procedures or devices that might be used in the workplace. It might be a challenge to make him feel motivated to deviate from the standard protocols that he was introduced to when he started working in some area.

It is difficult for people to change their attitudes or be motivated differently by their senses experience things for the first time. The first impressions make a difference in how someone sees things. This is why when businesses train employees, they always expose them initially to key principles that they should follow and various rules.

The Development of the Brain

Studies and scans have found that the frontal lobe is responsible for the brain to develop and promote certain behaviors. When the frontal lobe is activated, people have a strong interest in actions. The subcortex of the brain will trigger sensations relating to whether certain behaviors or experiences are pleasant or distressing.

As these two areas are supported, the brain will identify ideas and concepts relating to pleasure. When certain forms of pleasure occur, people want to feel happy and confident.

The Development of Neurotransmitters and Hormones

When the brain gets enough dopamine, it is easier for a person to feel motivated. The brain has to develop appropriately so that it is easier for dopamine to be produced. This includes the proper formation of the frontal and subcortex of the brain. Additional hormones have to be produced to support the development of various motivational actions:

1. Testosterone influences the sexual motivations of a person. This includes the potential for someone to be aggressive in some way.

2. Estrogen triggers the emotional behaviors that a person might experience. It influences the overall motivations one holds based on certain feelings and produces a sense of appreciation.

3. Oxytocin impacts sexual and social behaviors and regulates anxieties. It might help with managing how comfortable and motivated a person is when falling in love.

As the brain evolves, these hormones will trigger many factors that impact one's motivation. Testosterone and estrogen are hormones that are associated with the male and female bodies. Although a male's body does produce a small amount of estrogen, it is testosterone that dominates the mind. The development of testosterone often encourages a male to engage in physical activities and sometimes have more violent or aggressive thoughts and behavior.

For women, the development of estrogen makes them more likely to be caring and loving to others. This includes a focus on some emotional parts of life. Like with men, women do have some testosterone but it is not as prevalent.

The development of the brain and how it produces those hormones will directly influence the motivations that people have. In fact, the motivations that people have changed as those hormones are reduced in intensity. As a person ages, their body becomes less likely to produce gender-based hormones. These changes influence what people do in their lives and how they act and respond to other people.

Chapter 23 – Piaget's Values for Cognitive Development

Part of the development of motivation in the brain is how a person's cognitive functions develop. This concept of cognitive development was explained in the mid-20th Century by the Jean Piaget. His theory is that the human brain develops in a certain order in four particular stages. The brain has to develop through these stages for it to change.

This can be noticed when considering how children develop and what motivates them to act in certain ways. Schools can use Piaget's theory to understand how to reach children as they age and help them feel motivated enough to learn.

This may also be considered when looking at how adults are motivated. Adults often think more about how well they can handle certain concepts based on what they notice. It takes the experience to develop a logical understanding of the concepts and ideas that they want to work within their lives. By understanding cognitive development, it explains how a person might have a delayed sense of understanding logic.

Four Key Stages

Piaget explains that the brain develops through four stages.

1. Sensory and motor development

The first stage occurs from birth and will develop to be able to differentiate their self from other objects. A child will notice that he or she is capable of causing many actions, thus leading to many intentional actions. The motivation might be just to see what happens next.

A child will experience object permanence for the first time. That is, the child will notice that things will continue to exist when out of sight. For instance, a child will know his mother is somewhere else even though not in his line of sight. This marks the first step in a child's ability to handle logic and to recognize how things act and work in the real world.

2. Pre-operational

The pre-operational stage occurs when a child is at least two years of age to about seven years. A child learns to use language as a means of representing different concepts. The child does not see other peoples' viewpoints, thus leading to a self-centered form of motivation where the child's interests are the only things that the child can focus on.

It is also at this time when the child starts to notice how certain things might be similar to each other. For instance, a child will no longer see a bunch of blocks in one big pile. The child will see red blocks, green blocks, and white blocks. That child can easily distinguish between them and place all of the similar blocks into a group. Being able to identify individual ideas is the second major development in a child's ability to think logically.

3. Concrete Operational

The concrete operational stage occurs at the age of seven to eleven. The child will start to think logically and have an objective sense of understanding. Items can be distinguished by multiple characteristics and not just by one.

In terms of motivation, a child will start to notice that there are consequences that come with certain actions. The child will have to think about how certain motivations might impact other people and how relationships with those people might change. The potential for a child to be impulsive and ready to do things without thinking twice will start to decline.

4. Formal Operational

The final stage is reached at the age of eleven and will persist throughout one's life. A person will use more logical thought for certain concepts and may be able to predict what might happen in the future. As the formal operational functions develop, the child will learn the difference between right and wrong. The child will put more thought into the motivational process and understand what might be appropriate and what is not.

As one becomes older, logical thought is necessary. Through experience, new logical concepts and beliefs are established. All of these thoughts and concepts have to be applied throughout one's life to produce a better understanding of what one can expect. This includes knowing how certain values can be applied.

By using these four stages, a person can recognize that the things they do have consequences. Knowing one's actions have possible consequences is essential to avoid severe consequences and punishment in order to live an active, productive, and safe life.

The Development of Ethics

Piaget's theory explains the evolution of the brain and that it takes some time for people to understand ethics when it comes to their motivations. Those who evolve and develop will fully understand that there are always two sides to any issue. These include concepts that focus on what people might understand and on how others feel about certain situations.

Motivation can be influenced by how someone's sense of ethics develops. When a child does not have a full understanding of ethics, that child is motivated to do things solely for their own benefit. As a person ages, motivation evolves toward understanding the requirements that all people in a certain situation have. By knowing how others in a situation will act, a person will be motivated to help everyone involved.

For instance, a young boy of five years of age might ask to play with a rubber ball that another child owns. That boy might want to play with the toy, but he is not fully aware that it is not his possession. He does not have the ethical consideration at this point to recognize that it is wrong for him to take something that clearly does not belong to him. As that child gets older and has more experiences, he begins to notice that it is not good for him to take someone else's toys without asking the owner for permission. Eventually, the boy will see that he should either play with his own toys or learn to share.

As an adult evolves, they will start to use the lessons they have learned while growing up. The same man who years earlier learned about sharing and asking for permission might think carefully about what could happen when he sees a particular item in the workplace that he needs for completing a task. He might ask if there is a form he has to fill out to rent something that he could use for a certain task.

This is a unique psychological concept that shows how one's brain might change. The ethical values that one holds will make a difference as a person will start to think about the good and bad things that might develop as consequences.

However, this does not mean that a person will always be motivated by ethics. There are often times when the motivations revert back to self-centered thoughts where no one else is considered. In those cases, this might happen if a person is trying to do things to simply avoid trouble.

Chapter 24 – Self-Determination Theory

Self-determination is defined as having the personal ability to make a decision without having to seek affirmation or approval from another person.

Self-determination theory is a relatively new concept as it was only introduced in the 1990s. It is also a valuable part of motivation as it concentrates on the three innate psychological needs.

The Three Basic Needs

The self-determination theory states that three important needs exist for a person to survive. These may directly impact the motivation that one has.

Competence

First, a person must have the competence to make the right decisions. When a person is competent, they can master an outcome and control one's environment. A person is more motivated to do things when they are competent to complete a task. People who are not competent would have a difficulty completing certain tasks they might be expected to complete. They might not know why something needs to be done or understand the rules involved. A person who is not competent will not have the motivation to do a task.

The best way for a workplace to help a person acquire competency is to offer enough instruction to do a task. This could include a series of instructions about new concepts being introduced.

Relatedness

Relatedness refers to how close a person is to others. This includes relationships with family members, siblings, parents, co-workers, neighbors, etc. It is often easier for a person to feel motivated when many of these people are involved. Those people will make an impact on whatever someone is contemplating doing.

Decisions are made to encourage strong relationships with others. A person has a need to feel close to others and to make sure those people are treated carefully to keep those people protected. A worker might be motivated to earn money because that money can be used to help pay for food and shelter for family members, for example. As those needs are met, the worker will have a sense of belonging.

People who are removed from a concept of a task will not have the motivation to finish the task. Those people will feel as though a concept is too foreign to them and not intriguing. As a person is experienced with new concepts, those things become a little easier for a person to feel comfortable with. Therefore, it might be best for a person to be given a bit of time to learn about the new concepts or procedures they have to use. It becomes easier for a person to develop a sense of relatedness when that person starts to recognize what is needed to complete a task and knows the concepts involved.

Autonomy

People prefer to have control over their own lives. They want the ability to make the right choices about what they want to do. It is through autonomy that people are motivated.

Autonomy does not mean that a person can do just anything. There are still limits as to what someone can do based on certain laws or rules. Autonomy gives a person a sense of free will. That person acts based on their interests or values within reason and is based on what is available and what can be legitimately done at a given time.

The brain might start to feel comfortable with being controlled. This challenge to autonomy might persuade a person might stop thinking about the difficult issues. By thinking more about how particular changes might develop and how to follow instructions, it might become easier for that person to feel confident in what is being introduced.

The three parts of the self-determination theory combine to allow a person to do things that they have control over while also having enough support from others. By having free will while also being influenced by other people and knowing the consequences of actions, people will have the freedom to make decisions. They will feel motivated by the knowledge that they are free spirits who are capable of doing what they feel is right.

How This Links to Intrinsic and Extrinsic Motivation

Intrinsic Motivation

A vital part of what makes the self-determination theory so important is that it focuses on both intrinsic and extrinsic motivation. In the case of intrinsic motivation, a person focuses on the enjoyment and satisfaction that comes with completing a task. A person will be fully self-determined and in control of one's mind.

Intrinsic motivation creates a calm approach to learning. There is no sense of competition involved with other people nor are there any worries associated with assets like money or other special rewards. A person will think more about the excitement that comes with learning new ideas. As those concepts are explored and eventually used, it becomes easier for someone to evolve and stay with the concepts one is being taught without challenging any perceptions or other concepts.

Extrinsic Motivation

For extrinsic motivation, the level of self-determination is based on how the motivation is regulated. There are four aspects of extrinsic motivation:

1. Integrated regulation

A person will feel the most self-determined. The awareness of the situation is the most important part. As the person knows what is happening, they become more likely to want to help someone else. It is not a process derived from self-satisfaction but rather from the awareness of how the actions will affect others.

2. Identified regulation

The motivation will be generated by the personal importance that comes with the task. It may take some extra time for a person to realize what the full value of something they are doing.

3. Introjected regulation

Self-determination begins to decline and it becomes harder for a person to want to do things without a reward attached to it. While there are still some internal benefits that might motivate a person, the punishments for not performing become more important as a motivating factor.

4. External regulation

A person will not be influenced by their internal thoughts. It will be the outside rewards and punishments that will make a greater impact. A person might become dissatisfied with the emotional or mental aspects of working on a task, but would be motivated by the need to comply.

The self-determination theory is a necessity to see how people are motivated based on their determination and how that determination will change over time. The might create a great impact on what one wants to do in life.

Chapter 25 – The Concept of Positive Psychology on Motivation

One of the most important goals that any person might have in life is to find ways to become happy and confident. When a person feels positive and upbeat about life, there will always be something to look forward to when one is happy. To get there, a person has to put in a strong effort to find solutions to obstacles and find success.

Positive psychology focuses on what makes life worthwhile. It is about the positivity that comes with life and how people can get to the ultimate goal of being happy.

Motivation is easier to find with a positive. Positive psychology states that when a person feels confident about something, it becomes easier for that person to stay motivated. That person's performance will improve while the enjoyment of the job will be greater.

Concentration on the Will

Motivation has been interpreted as being a product of one's connections with other people or from threats or needs that someone might have. Positive psychology places a stronger emphasis on a person's will. This refers to the desire that a person has to master a certain field of work or to complete tasks of interest. The desire or will that a person has makes it easier for that person to feel motivated. This is more powerful and influential than a reward or the ultimate goal of finishing a task.

Those who have a strong will are always ready to do what they can to evolve and change their lives for the better. When the will is strong, it becomes harder for a person's attitude to change. Fortunately, a powerful will should produce motivation to continue efforts to continue a task for as long as it takes.

A Focus on Holism

Holism is a part of positive psychology that can be used to determine how well someone might work and considers that person as a whole - the mind and body working together.

Personal growth is the most important part of holism. When a person grows mentally, the entire self will feel more confident and at ease. This allows for happiness as there is a better sense of certainty within one's life. That certainty will lead to success because of how productive and active someone might be about particular points in life.

When the mind and body seem to be at odds, that person will have to find out what is keeping him or her from feeling motivated and to then find a solution for the problem and find motivation again.

How People Can Attain Positivity

People who have studied positive psychology, particularly Maslow, found that there is a potential for anyone to become confident and happy with life in general. Those who understand what they are doing and are not fearful will feel motivated. Happiness is critical for allowing someone to be ready and willing to continue working.

Several behaviors help a person become positive and confident:

1. The right growth choices have to be made.

A person might choose to grow instead of remaining in the same position afraid of what might happen weeks, months, or even years down the road. It is through positive thinking that a person can realize that there is something worth doing in life and that there is no real reason to panic.

This relates to developmental psychology in that a person will learn how to make the right choices. When someone discovers logic and recognizes what actions might be wrong, it allows that person feel confident with the actions they have chosen.

2. Honesty is the best policy.

People will always have doubts about the decisions they face. When someone is honest and realistic about certain actions and events, that person will be able to think about the positive things that come with making certain decisions.

Being dishonest is often a concern for many people. The mind of a dishonest person becomes preoccupied with trying to keep a lie running for as long as possible. This might reduce a person's productivity due to the worry and stress that comes with keeping up a certain image. When a person is honest, they will become happier and confident because they are working based on the realistic expectations and situations without having to create a charade that is not real.

3. A person will have to stop being defensive.

Positive psychology recommends that people avoid being defensive. When a person continues to defend their actions, they do not consider realistic consequences of certain actions. By not being defensive, a person will stop thinking about negative things that might happen.

This also helps to develop empathy for others. As someone becomes empathetic and starts to understand the views of other people, they can become productive. That person will stop focusing on the differences one has with others and will concentrate on what someone can do to increase one's skills and become more powerful.

Being defensive can make it harder for someone to get along with other people and prevents them from asking for help.

4. Impulse voices are more important than introjected voices.

Introjection is a process where a person thinks about the voices of other people. A person might introject those voices and assume that others are going to be judgmental when, in reality, the person is not going to be judged by others.

Impulse voices are different because they occur at random within one's own mind. These positive voices are more active and are not judgmental. They give someone the belief that by taking some action they will succeed and have a better life.

The impulse voices should be considered if the voices are realistic and do not have any potentially dangerous consequences. The goal is to have a positive result.

The development of logic and reasoning allows impulse voices to be heard. A person might start to notice that certain impulse voices are realistic and offer sensible ideas. Others might be pessimistic and focus on illegal or potentially harmful actions. It is up to a person who hears these voices in their mind to make the correct decisions. It is easier to make those choices as the brain develops and becomes more rational and knows what makes a decision appropriate.

5. Anyone who wants to move forward must be open to the experiences being produced.

Positive psychology places an emphasis on people being open to new ideas. This includes considering new concepts. By lowering one's defenses, it becomes easier for those new experiences to happen.

Those who are happy will not be afraid and will be curious. They will notice that the world has many positive things for them to explore.

Positivity is always important for the workplace as it directly impacts how productive and successful someone might be. Knowing how to stay positive and upbeat about anything that comes along in the workplace is a necessity for keeping a business successful and thriving.

The Actualizing Tendency

The next aspect of positive psychology involves the actualizing tendency. This is considered to be the desire that a person has for enhancing their life. It is a continuous tendency to keep moving toward strong goals without worrying about the risks that may develop. Those who follow the actualizing tendency will be more likely to grow and advance as people. A person will want to keep accepting new challenges and will be motivated to go toward new things that might not normally be considered.

The important part of this tendency is that it is not something a person will immediately notice. Rather, it is evidenced by the behaviors and how much time it takes for someone to enter into those actions. Businesses can identify employees who have this tendency by noticing how those people might be willing to work and how they are not afraid to move into certain actions in as little time as possible.

Resistance levels may be studied when looking at how the actualizing tendency works. Those who resist certain things are less likely to possess this tendency. Those people might be fearful of change or new ideas and might simply become unhappy. When someone has the actualizing tendency, they will welcome challenges and change.

Organismic Valuing Process

The organismic valuing process can be used to identify how a person can grow and thrive. Organismic valuing focuses on the tendency for a person to be ready and willing to learn new things or to take part in actions they are not familiar with.

The organismic valuing process could be used to identify how certain actions in the workplace might take place. A secretary might notice that she could work extra hours to help manage a new database or to update the infrastructure within that database. She begins to notice that the action will be to her benefit and to the company's benefit as well. Her actions will indicate that she is a reliable employee who is willing to learn something new and help her employer. She will also make it easier for the employer to complete certain tasks.

The valuing process shows that there is a benefit involved in the process for every person involved.

By following organismic valuing, the person becomes aligned with good values. More importantly, the natural attitude that someone has for handling certain tasks will be stronger. The risk of self-questioning behaviors will decline as it is harder for someone to be frustrated or worried about the tasks at hand.

<u>Vital Principles</u>

For the organismic valuing process includes necessities that focus on many concepts that make life easier and continues to evolve into adulthood:

1. A person must be authentic.

Authenticity is being true to the self. It shows that a person genuinely wants to work with a certain concept and prefers to move forward with a sense of comfort and happiness.

2. A sense of autonomy can be established.

Positive thinkers are motivated when they are capable of making their own decisions. When autonomy is involved beneficial and positive decisions will be made almost automatically and without any dispute over whether or not they are valuable.

3. All judgments are to be based on one's own assumptions or values.

People who do not think positively will focus more on the values or assumptions that other people have. A sense of independence in making decisions is more important. This sense of control makes it easier for the right choices to be made without suffering from a judgment in the process.

4. There should never be an assumption that there is a definite end-game.

Positive thinkers always believe that the human mind is always evolving. They do not have a singular direction with an end goal in sight. By focusing more on natural evolution and continued growth, it is easier to stay motivated and successful.

There exists the belief that no one is going to be judged for the decisions they make.

5. Good relationships are to be established.

When the right relationships happen, people will understand each other and comprehend the needs that they have. It becomes easier for people to stay positive in the workplace as there will be fewer arguments. Those in strong relationships will be on the same page and will know the rules of the workplace and how to resolve issues that may develop.

Positive psychology will make a great impact on how a business thrives and what will make it change and improve. Happiness allows everyone to thrive and develop in a positive way. The excitement of moving forward and getting something extra out of work is always positive.

Chapter 26 – The Principle of Utility

The principle of utility is a part of psychology is that people are motivated to help others. The concept was introduced in the 10th Century by John Stuart Mill. He theorized that people must engage in actions designed to provide people with happiness. A person should be motivated to allow others to grow and to make them feel confident and to become.

This is a form of positive psychology that motivates people into feeling that anything can be done so long as there will be a good result as long as everyone involved will benefit. There are many restrictions and regulations about what one can do at a certain time.

How Utility Works

Here's a good example. A manager might want to get his employees to feel positive about their work. He might consider many solutions to help his employees feel positive. He could consider holding a special after-hours party so that all the people in the workplace can talk with each other.

He could also offer special bonuses to people who perform well or even pay extra to those who work for a certain number of hours in a week. Some employees who have been with the company could be given bonuses for their loyalty. Whatever the case is, the manager will do what he can legitimately do to help others.

The utility is a part of positive psychology that concentrates on happiness. If used appropriately, it becomes easier for people to thrive and feel confident about the work that they are doing. In this example, the employees will benefit and be happy about what the manager proposes. The manager will be happy knowing that he is finding a way to help others while also doing something that will benefit him and the company as well.

What About Resources?

A fact of life involves aiming to get as many resources as possible. Those who can attain more in their lives will have an easier time enjoying what they have. There is a belief among many that they are happier when they have more assets. This includes more money, more possessions, and more freedom. For instance, when someone has enough money, they can easily handle their expenses and to acquire the basics needed for a comfortable life. Having money, allows a person to be happy. This relates to the principle of utility based on how those who use their resources to do right by others.

The principle of utility infers that people use whatever resources they have to make others happy. For instance, a person who is wealthy might consider giving bonuses to other people at the same workplace. That person might also provide a charitable donation to some organization that they support.

A person should be responsible and careful with their resources. This includes knowing how to use them in a carefully controlled and managed manner. By knowing how to use resources properly, a business will grow and thrive.

Different from Hedonism

Although the principle of utility might sound like hedonism, utility actually focuses on a more realistic approach. Hedonism is criticized for being self-indulgent and selfish. A person who is hedonistic focuses on pleasure above all else while sacrificing many things for self-indulgence.

The principle of utility is a more realistic approach to living. It acknowledges that there will be pain and difficulty in life. It is up to a person who lives the concept of utility to provide a way to resolve disputes or issues.

The utility is based on certain sanctions. Hedonism operates with no sanctions. Hedonistic people are concerned with pleasure without considering they will become repulsive or unattractive to others.

Appropriate Sanctions

Mill argues that the principle of utility uses two types of sanctions to ensure that pleasure is managed appropriately. These sanctions keep utility from being similar to hedonism:

1. External sanctions

Outside sanctions are what people might think. These include the legal punishments people might be subjected to and social disapproval. External sanctions define the limits of people's actions. People will have to find ways to establish pleasure without breaking laws or committing actions that might be shunned by the public and considered as being selfish.

For instance, people can consider donating funds to charitable organizations or even support renovations in their workplaces to create work environments that encourage positive feelings. A manager might even offer special vacation pay to people who have worked a long time. The positive actions will motivate people to continue working.

2. Internal sanctions

The internal sanctions are the feelings a person has. A manager might be afraid of alienating employees, thus prompting him or her to establish open house events so that people in the workplace can get to know each other while off the clock in a casual and relaxed environment.

The goal of these sanctions is to keep people from being judged by others while also making sure everyone in the workplace is comfortable.

It is up to any business or individual to watch for how the principle of utility may be used. This aspect of positive psychology has its limits as people will have to think about the sanctions that are involved. Although the overall goal is to be happy and to encourage positive feelings in others, the principle will be difficult to manage if it is not used the right way.

Chapter 27 – The Instinct Theory

People develop in many ways regarding how they might think and act. It is the instincts that people have that are truly unique. These instincts develop over time. Instinctual actions are not learned intentionally. They are an action that people will engage in without thought or planning.

Instinct is specifically defined as being a fixed form of behavior that someone might regularly engage in. A person will respond in a specific manner based on certain stimuli. The specific stimuli vary based on the situation.

The instinct theory of motivation states that all people are born with certain tendencies that cause them to do certain things when presented with particular events or stimuli. This is the belief that people will engage in certain actions no matter what other things might happen.

The behaviors that follow the instinct theory are not necessarily learned. It is often difficult to discover what might cause a person to engage in a certain way. One point for certain about instinct is that it is a dynamic point of human behavior.

Instinct is not something that can be easily controlled. Managers in workplaces can attempt to discover what causes people to act in certain ways, but to unveil instinct is always a challenge.

An Example of Instinct

To understand how instinct is related to motivation, it helps to take a look at an example. In most cases, the instincts that someone has will cause that person to engage in some action immediately. The best example can be seen through the work of Konrad Lorenz, a famous 20th Century ethologist. He studied young geese after they hatched. He noticed that the geese would become physically and emotionally attached to the first thing that they saw after their birth. In most instances, the geese would be attached to their mother. However, in this case, Lorenz was the first thing that those birds noticed. As a result, the geese became attached to him.

Instinct shows how it might impact one's behavior and ability to act in a certain way. Most importantly, that person acting on instinct does not think twice about a behavior. The motivation is inherent and natural.

It is not fully clear how long it takes for certain instincts to develop. Instincts may also develop not long after birth and will cause any person who experiences them to act in unique ways that are different from what most might expect. Instincts last a lifetime and will be impossible to control.

Basic Considerations

Famed psychologist William McDougall found that instincts are behaviors that are unlearned and are always expressed in the same way. Those instincts are natural among all figures within the same species. Each of the instincts focuses on behavioral actions and on managing one's emotions while perceiving certain behaviors or threats.

In particular, McDougall found that there are many kinds of instincts that people have that will directly influence how a person might behave in a certain way:

- The need to be with a parental figure

- A desire for comfort

- Cravings for sex

- Physical hunger

- A sense of curiosity

- A need to have some positive feelings in one's life; this might come from laughter

Some behaviors people express in public or in the workplace are often based on their instincts. Let's say that a worker in an office might be near a copy machine. He might start to toy around with the digital menu display. He could look around to see what menus exist and what settings can be controlled within that machine. This is all to satisfy his instinctual curiosity. He simply wants to see how the machine works; nothing else motivates him at the time.

The important point is that instinct is often the ultimate form of motivation. It is a type of behavior that a person will engage in immediately without thinking. A person will quickly partake in instinctual behaviors because there is a need to engage in such an act.

Differing Concepts

Instinct theory is a part of the motivation that involves natural values and actions:

1. Freud's argument of life or death

Sigmund Freud's belief is that instincts are often driven by the life or death issues. There are two kinds of instincts in his view. The life instincts relate to general survival, reproduction, and satisfaction. When a person has these motivations, it becomes easier for that person to use one's instincts to be positive.

Freud also argues that death instincts are common among people. He states that people unconsciously are curious about death and wonder what happens after one's death. The life instincts that people have are always going be stronger to keep people from engaging in those death instincts. When a person is no longer motivated to work toward those life instincts, they will eventually move away from wanting to live and will have a depressive attitude.

2. James' belief of survival

William James has a different idea of the instinct theory. James believes that instincts are often designed with survival in mind. He states that many instinctual behaviors will cause people to become defensive. People might have instincts relating to the fears which cause them to be angry toward other people. The goal is for people to think about what they can do to stay positive and happy with one another and with themselves. James believes that instincts are vital for people to escape from being harmed and that those instincts will kick in when any perceived threats occur. This is much different from Freud's theory about instincts triggering desires for life and death.

3. Meyers' sense of consistency

Psychologist David G. Meyers argues that an instinct is a behavior that is fixed or constant. That is, the instinct will cause a reaction the same way every single time it is expressed. He references the instincts that infant children have as a good example of this. An infant has a reflex that causes the child to find and suck on a mother's nipple. This is a behavior that the child does not learn but simply engages in; it is also consistent among all children at this early stage in life.

Two Major Problems Surrounding the Instinct Theory

Although the instinct theory might help identify what causes people to be motivated, there are two issues to be aware of.

First, although many people share certain instincts within a species, not all people are going to express the same behaviors. For example, people might assume that all women are going to have strong maternal instincts when they take care of their children. In reality, not all women have the instinct that they need to be the best possible parents. This is a point that directly challenges Meyers' belief of how instincts have to be consistent. However, it might just be that Meyers' theory works mainly for infants and other young children whose brains have not developed.

Second, there might be cases where certain emotions will interfere with a person's instincts. A person might start to think that they must absolutely engage in certain behaviors because that person is jealous of someone or may be desperate to make a difference in some way. Those feelings might keep instincts from actually being used. This would make it impossible to actually predict what someone would do at a given moment.

There is also the related belief that individual histories might influence how they manage their instincts. People might have their own specific beliefs or attitudes that they have learned throughout their lives regarding certain concepts or behaviors. They might act in their own particular ways because they depend on behaviors that they have learned based on prior events in their life.

Is It Possible for People to Control Instincts?

One question that many people, especially those who run their own businesses, might have is whether or not there is a possibility to control the instincts that other people have.

The good news is that the human mind has evolved over the centuries and it is not hard to identify what causes certain people to engage in specific actions. A person might be motivated based on what others in a local area might be doing and what situations are in a local area. The human mind can use common sense to identify when instinctual behaviors are expressed. For example, it is easy to see that a person might run away from a snake because that person instinctually feels that the snake would be a threat.

Rational Thought

The mind has evolved so that some instincts can be potentially controlled. A person's instincts can be controlled by informing that person of consequences that might come about when those instincts are allowed to take over.

In a workplace, a person might let a worker know that one's instinctual sense of curiosity might be a threat in some instances. Warning signs might be placed on electrical materials to let people know the danger and to stay clear of those items. This ensures that one's instinctual behavior is curbed. In this case, the change will focus on being more cautious and in control of what one might be thinking or doing in a certain environment.

Curbing an instinct works provided that the brain has evolved enough to support thought and understanding. The brain must have established enough connections to determine when it is fine for certain instincts to take over and when they should be suppressed.

Analysis of Past Actions

In many cases, the human brain can be controlled by allowing a full analysis of any actions one has engaged in. For instance, a person in the workplace could be consulted about events that they engaged in as a result of instinctual behaviors. A person's behaviors might include that person playing with a printer's settings out of curiosity. That person might be told that their actions caused the printer to malfunction. This could lead the person to realize that maybe it is not a good idea to exercise their curiosity just to see what happens.

It is not going to be as easy to manage the instincts when trying to influence how a person is motivated. The instincts that people make it harder for people to think twice. By careful analysis, it might be easy to discover what instincts are being engaged in and predict what might happen.

Instincts can at least be curbed in some way. When the instincts one wishes to follow are fully understood, it becomes easier for a person to thrive and expand one's horizons.

Chapter 28 – Drive-Reduction Theory

While the instincts that people have are important for determining how they are motivated and to predict what causes such motivation to develop, drive-reduction theory may play a role in understanding how people might act in various situations according to their needs.

Sometimes the instincts that people have are based on those needs. There are many basic needs like the need for food, shelter, sleep and many others. People are frequently motivated by their desires to have those needs met.

The drive theory states that a person will need to satisfy the needs that they have in their daily lives if they are to stay protected and to maintain a consistent state of homeostasis.

Drive-reduction theory is a concept that Clark Hull proposed in the 1940s. It suggests that motivation comes about as people try to find ways to manage their biological functions and satisfy the basic needs that they have. A person will have a greater drive to do something when there is a perceived imbalance in one's life. When the imbalance is resolved, that drive is reduced as the person begins to feel confident and comfortable with their situation and less likely to struggle with any stresses in the process.

This chapter explains the drives that people have and how imbalances might be interpreted. A small imbalance may still trigger worries in a person's mind that will keep them from being able to perform regular functions or actions in a sensible or controlled fashion.

Understanding the Drive

The drive that a person has is the motivation to engage in a specific action. A person might have certain drives that focus on biological impacts. Drives often are a need to find shelter, have a partner for companionship or sex, or a need to earn money. The strongest drives produce the fastest actions. These are harder to stop or control than other motives.

A drive is trying to survive in the world. When a person follows a certain drive, they will want to continue behaving in some way based on the drive that is established. A drive allows a person to have a better and more confident life, but at the same time, the drive might cause a person's better judgment being clouded.

What Is Homeostasis?

Homeostasis is where a person is able to manage their internal environment to have a sense of stability. When a person is hungry, that person will have the drive to eat. After the hunger is satisfied, that person enters a state of homeostasis where there are no worries about food.

When a person is capable of retaining homeostasis, it is not hard for that person to feel positive. That person is not preoccupied with issues. The motivations that the person had early on will be fully managed and kept under control.

The brain itself might also trigger feelings of being in a state of homeostasis. When the brain notices that the body is tired, the brain will signal that the body needs sleep. This causes a person to be preoccupied with rest. The brain's natural chemistry will make an impact as the brain produces the signals that have to be followed so that the person will have a positive and better-controlled mindset.

When homeostasis is disrupted, it becomes harder for a person to stay productive or motivated. At this point, a person might begin to think about satisfying certain needs. For instance, a person who has not had enough sleep will feel less motivated than others because they are tired. They will feel a disruption that requires sleep and comfort to restore a sense of homeostasis. Until that sense is fully restored, that person will not be productive and capable of doing things.

What Does Drive-Reduction Theory State?

Clark Hull explained drive-reduction theory as a unique concept relating to motivation. A person will develop certain needs as a state of homeostasis is disrupted. The brain will start to find a way to resolve the issue and to restore homeostasis. The drive that is produced will last for long as it is necessary. Emotional and mental tension will develop when a person is unable to get one's drive in check.

Drive motivates what people might do. When a person experiences a drive, their motivation will move immediately toward what one should do.

This is a point that can be noticed in many working environments. For instance, a person might be in a state of homeostasis when things in the workplace are running smoothly. However, there might be a sudden issue that occurs like a long line of customers waiting for service or a machine in the workplace breaks down. Such actions will disrupt the overall sense of homeostasis.

This leads to a drive where a person is motivated to want to find a solution to the problem. They might try to serve as many customers in line as possible and maybe ask for help to resolve the problem. For the other example, the person will want to resolve the issue of the broken machine so it can start working again. The motivation that the person has will expire as the state of homeostasis is attained once the problem in question is fixed.

An even better example of drive-reduction theory is a person's need to satisfy a feeling of thirst. Let's say that a person is thirsty all of the sudden. That person will feel motivated to find a drink of water. The need for water is a need that has disrupted one's personal state of homeostasis. The thirst becomes a source of tension that makes a person feel a need to resolve the issue in some way. When a person drinks water, the thirst will be managed to keep the issue from being a threat.

The theory can be illustrated in five simple steps:

1. There is a lack of homeostasis in an environment.

2. A need is developed due to the disruption of one's homeostasis.

3. A drive to satisfy that need develops.

4. The drive leads a person to feel motivated to act in some way.

5. After the drive is met, the person will return to a state of homeostasis.

This process can repeat over and over every time homeostasis is disrupted in some way. The greatest concern is that there is no way of predicting when homeostasis will be impacted or how long it might take for it to be restored. The important point is to address the disruption of homeostasis as soon as possible. Failing to take care of the issue will create enough of a distraction so that normal behavior or normal business cannot be possible.

Identifying Habits

People can use drive-reduction theory to identify the habits that people might have. These habits include ones that are triggered as a result of certain behaviors that people might be focused on. Habits might be formed based on the disruptions in the status quo that one is normally used to feeling.

Habits might develop as a person is simply used to certain actions over time. Whether they come from instinct or simply from things that a person has learned over time, they can make a dynamic impact on one's mind and behavior. When the right habits are formed, it becomes easier for people to recognize how they are behaving and what they can do to resolve any issues in their actions.

A Learning Point

Drive-reduction theory can be used to help understand how people learn and to plan or prepare for instances when certain issues occur.

When a person satisfies the drive and the newfound state of homeostasis exists for a little while, they will no longer feel an intense drive to do something. They will know that the action used to satisfy the drive is something that can be done again later. A person who learns that drinking water satisfies their thirst will have learned that drinking more water resolves the thirst that will occur at another time.

Knowing what to do ensures that future actions can be used. Workplaces can use this point by letting people know what they can do to fix certain problems that they encounter. A manager might post information on how people can resolve issues like when customers are problematic or when machines are not working. Using the drive-reduction theory can help give people the motivation needed to fix problems as they occur.

Being able to fix problems in the workplace allows a business to thrive and stay active. This can also help people to continue to earn money, thus satisfying a secondary drive that indirectly solves a primary drive. This leads to the next point.

Primary and Secondary Drives

There are two different types of drives that people have.

1. Primary drive – A desire to satisfy a specific biological need

Primary drives are what a person feels has to be resolved for survival. People may focus on their needs for satisfying hunger, the need for sleep, or other basic needs. A desire for companionship and sex are included in these primary drives.

These are the most important drives that people have. Each drive has to be satisfied first before anything else can happen. The key is to prevent someone from feeling distracted or disrupted due to problems relating to the primary drives.

2. Secondary drive – Something that focuses on one's status or image and is not necessarily required for survival

Some of the secondary drives that people have are a desire to earn more money or to be at a higher position in the workplace. An employee might have a secondary drive to keep on working toward resolving certain problems in the workplace or to simply get more recognition than others in the same area.

Clark Hull argues that the secondary drives that people have will actually impact the primary drives but not in a direct way. While a person might satisfy one's secondary drive to earn more money, the primary drives of hunger and rest will be satisfied because that person will have the money needed to acquire the food one requires and to pay for the costs associated with a home to keep oneself safe and comfortable.

In many cases, people are motivated to follow those secondary drives because of the primary drives. People might be motivated to earn money because they know that the money they earn can help them to get the food they need and to pay for their home.

The secondary drive can be a much stronger motivator than what one might have for long-term needs. The primary drive focuses on the basic needs that everyone has to satisfy. Understanding the secondary drives help identify what causes them to feel motivated, thus helping them to satisfy their primary drives.

As those secondary drives are formed, it is crucial for a person to handle the primary drives. Any secondary drive that is formed before a primary drive is satisfied could be controlled by planning.

Success In the Workplace

The secondary drives are the most important ones to identify when discovering how people might behave in the workplace. The right secondary drives must exist so a business can grow. For instance, a person might have a secondary drive to be more productive and efficient in the workplace in order to have a promotion. Another has a secondary drive that focuses on just having a good image in order to appear outstanding if he completes specific tasks when he is asked to complete them.

The people who have resolved all of their primary drives are also interpreted as being more productive. These are people who have their lives in order because they know what they want to do and how they will act.

Working With Many Drives

An interesting part of the motivation is that a person does not have just one drive. A person could have many secondary drives. For instance, a person might have a need to earn more money, to have a strong romantic relationship, and maybe to have one's ideas exposed to other people.

Motivation, in this case, concentrates on getting everything one wants. Those who have many drives will learn faster. A business could use this to train its employees to handle many tasks and watch for various parameters in the workplace.

There are no limits as to how many drives a person might have in one's life. Those who can handle many drives might be interpreted as being more motivated because they want to do many things. However, it might be very easy for their sense of homeostasis to be disrupted as it is very easy for someone with many drives to become disorganized and confused.

Any Issues?

There are some concerns relating to the drive-reduction theory. In particular, there are concerns that a person might cause others to be conflicted or upset when trying to satisfy their own drives. A person might aim to undermine others who get in the way of a need to reduce a drive.

Some people might have drives that focus on producing pleasure. This might actually be problematic to the drive-reduction theory in that the solutions produced are designed to satisfy the desires that people have. That is, people might use their drives to satisfy optional things or needs they do not need for survival. A person might have the drive to earn money for a vacation but not necessarily focused on survival. The money could be divided evenly between survival and pleasure. The drive-reduction theory does not necessarily place an emphasis on drives inspired by non-essential concepts in life.

The best way for a manager in the workplace to identify the drives of an employee could be to look at how that person is producing certain actions in the workplace. These include actions where primary or secondary drives are being followed. A manager might notice that a worker is focusing too much on the primary drives, thus keeping that person from being productive. A manager might choose to allow that worker to have some time off so they can get those primary needs in order. It might also require consultation to discover what is causing that person to not having those needs met. When the primary drives are uppermost for an employee, it becomes harder for managers to figure out what is happening in the workplace.

Will Anyone Ever Be Truly Fulfilled?

The last point about the drive-reduction theory is that it is a life-long part of the motivation that is never going to expire. The primary needs that people have are never going to disappear. People will become thirsty once again after a while, for instance. A secondary drive can be resolved quickly, but it will have to also provide for the primary drives to be satisfied.

All secondary drives vary based on how intensive they are and how much work is involved to satisfy them. Every drive that is produced should be planned. When planned correctly, it becomes easier for the theory to stay functional. When people are identified based on their drives, it is easier for others to identify who is the most motivated and therefore ready and willing to be productive.

Chapter 29 – The Social Psychology of Motivation

Social psychology focuses on how interactions between people will influence mental processes. Social psychology may be used to identify how motivated a person might be. Social psychology is not identical to positive psychology, but the end-game of the two fields is similar. The goal is to discover what it takes for people to feel better about themselves and capable of working on tasks without judgment. Social psychology concentrates encouraging people to do what they can to move forward and stay strong.

How Is Control Managed?

Social psychology focuses on how people are controlled by others. The perception of motivation changes when people notice that they are being controlled in different ways. It is through individual relationships that many situations might change and evolve.

Control might come about in one of two ways:

1. There might be several conditions within a relationship.

In this case, the motivation for keeping a relationship might be intense. This could happen when one person in the relationship is controlling and demands specific conditions to be met for the relationship continue.

As one person in a relationship is forced to comply and perform certain actions, it becomes a challenge for them to maintain motivation to stay focused and active in their work. The pressure from the complicated and difficult relationship will be too extreme for that person to be successful.

2. The relationship might be unconditional.

An autonomous feeling may develop so that the people who are linked to one another will be comfortable with each other. They will not feel judgmental about one another and will be accepting of any faults or flaws.

The positive nature of the relationship makes everyone feel more motivated. There are fewer stresses involved in the relationship. People will feel more successful because they know they are working hard to support one another without fear of being hassled or treated differently.

The second state is the one that most people want to achieve. When an unconditional relationship is achieved, it is easier for people to stay happy and motivated because fear in the relationship will not exist.

The Key Parts of Any Positive Relationship

Motivation is easier to support when a person has positive social relationships with others. It is through these relationships that it becomes easier for people to be accepting of others and what they want to do. This also allows people to stay motivated because of the powerful attitudes that develop.

There are five critical parts of a positive relationship that will influence how motivated a person might be. Each part concentrates on a different positive aspect that makes a social interaction stronger.

1. Warmth

A relationship needs a sense of warmth attached to it. People need to be there for each other while having a vibrant approach to their interactions. A strong sense of warmth is needed to allow a relationship to grow and be healthy.

For instance, a manager at a furniture store might treat his employees with care. He might show a sense of happiness whenever he gets into the workplace because he knows there is always going to be something good happening. When he feels dejected, it becomes harder for him to get the employees in the workplace to feel the same way. The greatest challenge at this point is to try and get people to have the desire to work.

2. Genuineness

The warmth developed in the relationship must also feel real. Genuineness refers to the recognition of a positive relationship. When a relationship is positive, it becomes easier for it to thrive.

The manager in this example might show a sense of warmth, but it will have to be genuine for it to be worthwhile. The manager might be trying to convince the employees that he is feeling positive and ready to do more for the workplace. However, he just might be frustrated with the furniture industry. He might feel as though his business is in trouble but does not want to admit it. This would lead him to project a false impression that he is happy. He could become nervous and agitated so that others in the workplace will quickly notice that something is wrong.

When that person is genuine in nature, he will be easier for the others in the workplace to take him seriously. Employees will know that the environment he is creating is a positive and happy one where everyone is encouraged to be themselves. This includes a lack of dread or worry.

3. Empathy

The two sides of a relationship need to respect each other's needs. When one person feels dejected, the other side should understand the concern and find a way to be sympathetic to that person's plight.

The furniture store manager, in this case, can talk with his individual employees about what they are feeling. One worker might say that she is nervous as this is her first job. The manager can talk with her and explain about his experiences with his first job and how nervous he might have been himself. By talking it over with the employee, an understanding is developed. The employee will see that she can perform to her best ability if she puts in the effort and abides by what the manager is telling her. She will also feel productive and motivated as she knows the manager she is working for genuinely cares for her and wants her to go far in this line of work.

4. Acceptance

There are always going to be differences between each party. These differences might be minimal, but sometimes they could be intense and difficult to surmount. It is through those differences that people are capable of expressing their greatest strengths as they care for others. By accepting people for how they are different, others feel cared for and recognized.

The manager might notice that some employees are different in their own ways. He might see that one person likes to be conversational with clients who want to buy furniture while another wants to talk about the features of the furniture in question. The manager will find ways to help each employee with their own strategies and conversational standards without being judgmental about how they are handling customers.

5. Confirmation

Both sides should know one another well enough so that they are not afraid to agree or disagree with one another. Confirmation is about respecting how different sides will act in certain ways and not be afraid of speaking one's mind. The friendly nature of one's actions can often be all that is needed for this part of running a business to work well.

How Can Social Relationships Improve?

The strongest social relationships are the ones where the parties involved feel the most motivated. Those relationships will become stronger when everyone involved works together and finds ways to keep a relationship positive.

Four particular strategies can be used to keep a relationship moving forward while motivating people to keep working to find solutions.

1. Those in a relationship can help each other and other people outside of that circle.

Motivation is easier to develop when people work harder to support each other. They will have a better understanding of what it takes for each other to be successful. It is even more important to provide help and support to people outside of the relationship.

The act of offering help to other people can take many forms. People can provide assistance by offering guidance to customers for finding items or learning how to use certain products or services. They may also train new employees to help them understand the job and recognize what they can do to be assertive.

By offering support for many people, it becomes easier for those in a relationship to know that their skills and abilities are worthwhile and are easy to support. It might also facilitate a social circle to grow.

2. Everyone in a relationship will have to understand what motivates each person.

Authenticity is a necessity for motivation. By knowing what triggers people to act in certain ways, people will also know what causes them to stay motivated. Being able to relate to others is easy to do when each party knows what makes the other positive.

It can take weeks or even months for people to get to know one another. This could require people to work for hours at a time together or just for people to have a few personal meetings or dates with each other. By continued involvement, they will discover how their efforts can be combined to create a stronger relationship and also be more productive and active.

3. The best relationship is one where people feel free to learn new things.

Learning is a continuous process for everyone in a relationship. By learning new things, everyone can be motivated as they know more about how they can live their lives and how they can improve what other people want to do in general. The experiences that people have from learning will foster positive feelings that all will feel comfortable adopting.

4. Each self will have to be properly defined.

Each person has their own definition of self. It is a collection of attributes relating to what someone is interested in, the skills a person has, and what they want in life. By having a clear definition of one's self, a person can grow and be productive.

Social psychology directly impacts many parts of motivation. It is all about understanding how people are motivated when they are in good, supportive relationships.

Chapter 30 – How Managers Becomes Leaders When Motivating People

It is important for managers in any work environment to notice how different people are motivated by different ideas. Managers are the representatives of a business who arrange for the right number of employees to be ready to accept any kind of task. A manager who wants to influence the motivations of people in the workplace can use many theories to get more out of their employees. That manager can eventually become a leader as a basic sense of leadership is established.

Focus on Achievements

The first way for a manager to become a leader is to think less about the results of tasks in the workplace and more on the achievements that follow. People are often focused on the results and how well someone might perform, but it is the achievements in the work environment that might be the biggest motivation.

A track and field athlete might be motivated to work harder to improve his times when running a long distance race. He might concentrate on the results and see when he is cutting a few seconds off his running times. Over time, he might start to look at achievements like qualifying for a major track meet or even winning the meet. He becomes more motivated as he focuses on the accomplishments that are more important than the results that are produced.

When a manager concentrates more on the possible achievements that someone can attain, it is easier for that manager to motivate people. The manager will let others know that there is a potential for valuable things to happen when achievements in the workplace are placed front and center above all else.

Creativity Is a Must

The next part of leadership is a focus on creativity. It is often easier for people to succeed and do the most when they can stay creative.

The problem with many managers is that they establish specific procedures and ideas that all people in a workplace have to use in order to keep the status quo intact. These concepts are not always appreciated by everyone as it is often hard for those processes to work constantly. It may also cause people to stop feeling motivated when they realize that some of the things they are doing are not necessarily working as well as they might have hoped.

A manager can motivate people by allowing them to be more creative in what they are doing and thoughtful over how certain actions can be supported. This relates to the Theory Y concept of motivation that was introduced earlier in this guide. By allowing people to feel motivated to create certain ideas and solutions, those people will want to keep on working. This improves the chances for people to enjoy what they are doing because they are personally invested in the job.

Listen Once In a While

One of the greatest problems that many people have with their managers at their workplaces is that they do not listen to their needs. They are often frustrated with how managers are not willing to hear them out over the problems that they might have. These include problems relating to how certain processes might be difficult or how new ideas could be used instead of some of the older ones.

A manager might make a business more productive and motivated by simply paying attention to the needs of their employees. A time could be could be established when the manager might be available in his office. This is similar to college campus professionals have regular hours for students to talk with them and ask for advice about certain things relating to their classes and projects. Simply listening to people and allowing them to get in touch with a supervisor or manager is often the best way to let people know that they are cared for while helping them to stay productive and successful.

Allow for Some Competition

It has always been believed that a bit of competition has never harmed anyone. Economists often argue that competition makes it easier for a community or work climate to move forward. People will feel encouraged to perform and to challenge themselves. Businesses might be motivated to produce distinct innovations that set them apart while encouraging the market or climate to evolve.

A manager could motivate employees by allowing them to be competitive and to challenge one another. The human mind is often equipped to handle the competitive nature of the workplace and to accept challenges. By working with the right level of competition, a business will thrive.

The competition should not be too intense. The competition includes something that allows people to see what they can do and how they might perform. The competition in question might be to see who can sell more of a certain product, complete more online tasks, or simply get enough people to sign up for a service that a company offers. The competition involved allows everyone to feel motivated and ready to work hard while still being realistic.

The manager's ability to get people in the workplace to feel motivated and encouraged to keep working is vital to a business' success.

Chapter 31 – What Causes People to Impair Motivation?

The overall goal of any workplace, school or other situation is to motivate people to act in certain ways. However, it is often a challenge for people to stay motivated. There may be some who might try to impair the motivation that others have.

It is challenging to even think about what causes a person to become negative. While no one likes it when a person wants to impair or inhibit motivation, there is always going to be a chance that someone will want to keep people from actually feeling motivated.

What is it that makes someone want to inflict harm? Why would a person go so far as to hurt other people by creating a negative environment? There might be some psychological answers to this. By addressing these issues, it might reduce the risk of further harm because of someone engaging in intentionally negative behaviors and actions.

Some people impair motivation often unintentionally. Psychological values suggest that people do not hurt people on purpose. Rather, they might think differently and not fully understand everything that makes people or certain concepts worthwhile.

Are People Naturally Evil?

The people who prevent others from being motivated are not naturally evil. A person is not born to be hostile to other people. Rather, people will begin to develop negative feelings based on the experiences they have.

For instance, a worker might try to keep people from wanting to complete a major renovation task at a work site. He might feel that the task is too dangerous and he will do anything he can to keep people from getting that task completed. This could all be as a result of a negative experience he had in the past. Maybe he was injured during a home renovation project. Perhaps he failed to complete a renovation task correctly and his property was damaged or lost its value. At this point, he will do anything he can to keep people from completing the renovation project.

The worker is not evil. He is simply trying to curtail the renovation because he feels that it is too risky. He is misguided in his thoughts and actions. He does not understand the true motivation for getting the task completed because the negative experiences he has had in the past are clouding his judgment.

A Lack of Empathy

Motivation may also be impaired by people not having empathy. For instance, a manager might want people to work overtime during a certain time of the year because he needs some major tasks at work completed. He might ask for this overtime because the season might be extremely busy.

There is a chance that the workers will not feel very motivated. They might feel stressed or overworked and therefore will not feel willing to work overtime. This is a problem for many workers that keep them from being motivated.

The manager is not intentionally trying to keep people from feeling motivated. Rather, he simply does not have the empathy needed to understand that his employees are not capable of handling the overtime that he wants them to do. Instead of thinking about changing schedules or hiring new employees to come in to handle the extra work, he feels that overtime is necessary.

In short, a person might not have the empathy needed to understand the problems that exist in the workplace. This is not intentionally misunderstanding. His insistence on overtime is the result of not having empathy for his workers.

A Lack of Oxytocin

Motivation is often impacted by a lack of oxytocin. Oxytocin is needed to help regulate one's thinking processes and will make it easier for people to see what is right versus what is wrong. When a person is in a stressful situation, the natural release of oxytocin in the body will be inhibited. The difficulty for the body to take in this chemical will make it harder for someone to feel empathy and a desire to help others. This, in turn, hurts the overall sense of motivation.

Oxytocin is often interpreted as a "trust hormone." It is a hormone that is produced when a person is near someone that they appreciate. In most cases, this happens when a person wants to establish a better romantic relationship with someone. As this neurotransmitter is produced, a person's positive feelings begin to rise. People typically associated oxytocin with sexual and romantic activities as it is more prevalent in the brain when a person hugs or kisses someone. It can develop when someone is near a person that they like even if it is not with romantic intentions in mind.

When the brain is unable to produce oxytocin, it becomes harder for a person to support others. This could be a real problem when a person tries to hold others back. This might be out of anger, but in most cases, it is due to lack of trust. This issue will keep people from being productive because they aren't receiving the help they think they deserve from other people in the workplace.

Too Much Oxytocin

Oxytocin can be just as dangerous as dopamine to one's psychological health if the brain produces too much of it. This is also why medications that promote the development of oxytocin are not provided to people often.

When a person develops too much of the hormone, that person starts to hold an attachment toward people who have certain characteristics. A person with an excess of oxytocin will express unintentional prejudices against people who are different in some manner. This stops a person from being capable of distinguishing between good and bad. Once again, the person who expresses those issues is not doing this on purpose and has no real idea that this problem exists.

The most important thing for people to notice when it comes to people harming anyone's sense of motivation is that it is almost always done unintentionally. A person might become stressed or pressured to the point where it is hard for that person to legitimately show a sense of empathy or care for others. The lack of empathy that comes with such a situation could also be a real problem.

Chapter 32 – Positives to Find In Any Motivational Plan

The psychological aspects of motivation focus on many points dedicated to helping people get the most out of their actions. It is necessary to look at how a motivational plan is working so the employees or students at a school might perform to their best potential.

The following is a list of positive aspects of any motivation plan to be effective.

Strong Involvement From a Leader

The person responsible for leading the employees in any situation should participate and offer a sense of support. This is to show that the efforts being promoted are legitimate and that the manager cares about the needs of everyone in the workplace.

A leader can make things a more personal by sharing his beliefs and values. Being direct and open to other people can show a human side. This allows people to understand that any efforts that a business is undertaking are managed in a realistic and logical manner.

What Rewards are Effective?

Rewards can be included in the motivational plan that is being introduced, but they must still be realistic and understandable. These could be bonuses, vacation days, or any other reward. The goal is to encourage productivity and have people work to their best capabilities to be entitled to the rewards.

For instance, a retail store might have a contest where people are challenged to get customers to sign up for a store-branded charge card. People could be offered a bonus for each signup while a larger prize is awarded to the person who has the greatest number of signups in a certain period of time. This allows people to work to their best abilities to reach the ultimate goal of convincing people to sign up for the service being provided.

This is a good way to encourage people to be productive, but the efforts should still be realistic. This can work only when the rewards are sensible and easy to attain if they put their minds to it.

Understand What Motivates Individuals

The most important point is what motivates a person in a situation. Although the theories listed here help to understand the psychological aspects of motivation, this does not mean that every theory is truly universal. There is always a chance that one or two or even more people in the workplace might have their own influences about the work they do. A manager needs to recognize that each person in the workplace will act differently from others and will have different motives for working.

When establishing a motivational plan, a business has to do more than just think about the psychological concepts that are involved. A business must also look into how well the campaign itself is working without being complicated.

Chapter 33 – A Few Final Points

Motivation is possible to instill in anyone because of the many ways psychological considerations can be put into place. To make motivation work even better, it is best for people to consider how they can stay motivated.

It is recommended that anyone who is serious about advancing oneself in life should take a look at what motivates them. The main purpose is to understand the benefits that can come with hard work.

A Need to Be Specific

As mentioned earlier, people will often be motivated by the needs that they have and what they might use to satisfy those needs. To truly be motivated, a person would have to be specific about the needs one has.

Articulating visions is a necessity. Someone cannot be motivated if they do not understand the specifics for what needs to be done at a given time. The visions one has should include where one wants to go, what they want to do, how that person will work, and what rewards are possible. By knowing more about what can be done, people will feel confident and aware of what they can do in any situation.

Analyze Fears

The fears that one has should be addressed in any potential situation. Every fear must be cataloged and reviewed to see if it is realistic or understandable. Sometimes a fear might be legitimate if it is about a person's inability to complete a certain task or one's immediate safety. With a further review, a person might notice that certain fears may be unfounded.

Intuition Is Vital

A person's intuition can influence what someone does. A person's intuition is often the most important thing because it directly impacts a person's ability to work and to stay productive. A person's gut might be more valuable at times. A gut feeling can cause a person to become motivated by realizing that there many positives and opportunities that can happen by initiating a certain action. By following such an action, a person may feel confident and motivated. The potential for significant hang-ups will be reduced when one's intuition is put into play. Intuition especially benefits people who time certain actions. Timing is critical in that a person who times their efforts will do more and produce more.

Keep Working Toward a Goal

The goals that a person sets up at the beginning of a task should be kept for as long as possible. While a person might feel that everything is done to attain a goal might become extremely hard to accomplish, that does not mean a person has to give up. Persistence is a vital part of the motivation that can influence how well someone can work on a task.

Keeping the goal in mind allows motivation to continue. When goals suddenly shift without any warning, it becomes harder for a person to stay motivated to accomplish a task. This is frustrating, but it is still essential to work toward a goal and to find a way to get to that end result as soon as possible. When the right amount of effort is expended to achieve a goal, there will be less confusion involved and therefore less frustration.

Do Not Become Overworked

People who feel overworked are more likely to lose their motivation. They might feel tired and incapable of going on.

Some might begin to see less benefit of the reward in the work they are doing.

Nurturing oneself is often the best way to keep the motivation for a task intact. People who are one-dimensional and focused on certain tasks will be less likely to feel comfortable and happy with their lives. By allowing for some relaxation and some time off, people will be refreshed and able to return to work with new vigor.

The options people have for nurturing themselves are diverse. People can choose to do things like take a walk in a park or visit a good friend. When a person relaxes, it becomes easier for the mind to feel comfortable. The stresses that come from a task will be a little lighter after a while. After a rest, there is a potential for a person to have inspirations to resolve certain problems or issues one might have.

Be Prepared

It is always a good idea to take a look at how certain benefits can be realized when a goal is reached. It helps to have a plan for what can be done after that goal is attained. A good idea is to invent a new goal that can be used.

By being prepared with a new goal, it becomes easier for a person to move forward with a certain plan and to feel confident about it. Those who are not prepared for what to do after a goal is reached will feel uncertain about what can be done next.

The Value of Visualization

Visualization is a part of psychology that many people use when finding a way to draw what they desire. When a person sees something, it is easier to attain it. Some might feel that by visualizing things, they can draw positive energy from something and therefore get what they want to come directly to them. This is also known as the law of attraction, but it might not work for every person.

One thing is for certain, and that is visualization can impact how a person plans. Visualization makes it easier for a person to look at how certain ideas can be implemented and plans made to actualize those ideas.

Allow for Flexibility

It is clear that the human mind is often willing to change and to listen to new concepts. The first things that a person learns might prove to be more important than anything else. The best thing for a business to do is to allow people to follow many paths to success or let them work as they see fit.

For instance, individual plans can work for those who operate under the Theory X pattern while those who follow Theory Y values might have their own standards. Meanwhile, the principle of utility may be used to allow people to feel happy with the rewards they are being offered provided that those rewards are being used within certain boundaries or acceptable limits. When the right plans are organized, a business can make its employees feel happy and confident.

Be Willing to Dream Big

The last thing for people to do when staying motivated is to never be afraid of the big picture. It never hurts to dream big and to think about the many things that can happen when enough effort is put into the work one needs to do. When someone thinks about all the great things that can happen in life, that person can stay active and ready to move toward a goal. Thinking big and beyond immediate goals will enrich one's life and give purpose to work.

Conclusion

It is fascinating to see how psychology has changed over the years. Practically any aspect of the human mind can be analyzed and reviewed. Looking at the different psychological theories can give insight into how people are motivated. There will always be a need to work hard toward motivating people and getting them to want to do their best in work situations.

By using the right psychological standards, businesses to help their employees feel confident about their work and their abilities. This includes helping them to feel motivated to be productive. When people are motivated right, the chances for a business to succeed will increase exponentially.

It is critical for managers to understand how the human brain works and how people have their own individual needs and wants. The patterns that are used for identifying how people are motivated and what causes them to act in certain ways should be explored in detail. Knowing what it takes to get the most out of employees is critical for a business to succeed.

Every business that wishes to work at its best potential must see what it can do when looking into the emotional and motivational needs that workers have. Knowing how to motivate them and what causes those people to be motivated is a necessity that helps a business to grow and thrive.

96276159R00127

Made in the USA
Lexington, KY
18 August 2018